W9-COU-686

PRACTICE – ASSESS – DIAGNOSE

180 Days of LANGUAGE for Fourth Grade

through the jungle

- ✓ capitalization
- ✓ punctuation
- ✓ parts of speech
- ✓ spelling

Author
Suzanne Barchers, Ed.D.

SHELL EDUCATION

Image Credits

All images Shutterstock

Standards

© Copyright 2010. National Governors Association Center for Best Practices and Council of Chief State School Officers. All rights reserved.

Shell Education

5301 Oceanus Drive
Huntington Beach, CA 92649-1030
http://www.shelleducation.com

ISBN 978-1-4258-1169-3

© 2015 Shell Education Publishing, Inc.

The classroom teacher may reproduce copies of materials in this book for classroom use only. The reproduction of any part for an entire school or school system is strictly prohibited. No part of this publication may be transmitted, stored, or recorded in any form without written permission from the publisher.

TABLE OF CONTENTS

INTRODUCTION AND RESEARCH

People who love the English language often lament the loss of grammar knowledge and the disappearance of systematic grammar instruction. We wince at emails with errors, such as when the noun *advice* is used instead of the verb *advise*. We may set aside a résumé with the incorrect placement of an apostrophe. And some of us pore (not pour) over entertaining punctuation guides such as *Eats, Shoots and Leaves* by Lynne Truss (2003). We chuckle over collections of bloopers such as *Anguished English: An Anthology of Accidental Assaults upon Our Language* by Richard Lederer (1987).

Even though we worry about grammar, our students arrive at school with a complex set of grammar rules in place—albeit affected by the prevailing dialect (Hillocks and Smith 2003, 727). For example, while students may not be able to recite the rule for where to position an adjective, they know intuitively to say *the yellow flower* instead of *the flower yellow.* All this knowledge comes without formal instruction. Further, young people easily shift between articulating or writing traditional patterns of grammar and communicating complete sentences with startling efficiency: IDK (I don't know), and for the ultimate in brevity, K (okay).

So, if students speak fairly well and have already mastered a complex written shorthand, why study grammar? Researchers provide us with three sound reasons:

1. the insights it offers into the way the language works

2. its usefulness in mastering standard forms of English

3. its usefulness in improving composition skills (Hillocks and Smith 1991, 594)

INTRODUCTION AND RESEARCH *(cont.)*

Studying grammar also provides users—teachers, students, and parents—with a common vocabulary to discuss both spoken and written language. The Assembly for the Teaching of English Grammar states, "Grammar is important because it is the language that makes it possible for us to talk about language. Grammar names the types of words and word groups that make up sentences not only in English but in any language. As human beings, we can put sentences together even as children—we all *do* grammar. But to be able to talk about how sentences are built, about the types of words and word groups that make up sentences—that is *knowing about* grammar."

With the publication of the Common Core State Standards, key instructional skills are identified, such as identifying parts of speech, using prepositional phrases, capitalizing, and correctly using commas. Writing conventions such as punctuation serve an important function for the reader—setting off syntactic units and providing intonational cues and semantic information. Capitalization provides the reader with such cues as sentence beginnings and proper nouns (Hodges 1991, 779).

The Need for Practice

To be successful in today's classroom, students must deeply understand both concepts and procedures so that they can discuss and demonstrate their understanding. Demonstrating understanding is a process that must be continually practiced in order for students to be successful. According to Marzano, "practice has always been, and always will be, a necessary ingredient to learning procedural knowledge at a level at which students execute it independently" (2010, 83). Practice is especially important to help students apply their concrete, conceptual understanding of a particular language skill.

Understanding Assessment

In addition to providing opportunities for frequent practice, teachers must be able to assess students' comprehension and word-study skills. This is important so that teachers can adequately address students' misconceptions, build on their current understanding, and challenge them appropriately. Assessment is a long-term process that often involves careful analysis of student responses from a lesson discussion, project, practice sheet, or test. When analyzing the data, it is important for teachers to reflect on how their teaching practices may have influenced students' responses, and to identify those areas where additional instruction may be required. In short, the data gathered from assessments should be used to inform instruction: slow down, speed up, or reteach. This type of assessment is called *formative assessment*.

 © Shell Education

HOW TO USE THIS BOOK

With *180 Days of Language,* students receive practice with punctuation, identifying parts of speech, capitalization, and spelling. The daily practice will develop students' writing efforts and oral reading skills.

Easy to Use and Standards-Based

These activities reinforce grade-level skills across a variety of language concepts. The questions are provided as a full practice page, making them easy to prepare and implement as part of a classroom morning routine, at the beginning of each language arts lesson, or as homework.

Every practice page provides questions that are tied to a language standard. Students are given opportunities for regular practice in language skills, allowing them to build confidence through these quick standards-based activities.

Question	Language Skill	Common Core State Standard
1	punctuation	**Language Standard 4.2**—Demonstrate command of the conventions of standard English capitalization, **punctuation**, and spelling when writing.
2	capitalization	**Language Standard 4.2**—Demonstrate command of the conventions of standard English **capitalization**, punctuation, and spelling when writing.
3–5	parts of speech	**Language Standard 4.1**—Demonstrate command of the conventions of standard English **grammar and usage** when writing or speaking.
6	spelling	**Language Standard 4.2**—Demonstrate command of the conventions of standard English capitalization, punctuation, and **spelling** when writing.

Note: Because articles and possessive pronouns are also adjectives, they are included in the answer key as such. Depending on students' knowledge of this, grade activity sheets accordingly.

HOW TO USE THIS BOOK *(cont.)*

Using the Practice Pages

Practice pages provide instruction and assessment opportunities for each day of the school year. Teachers may wish to prepare packets of weekly practice pages for the classroom or for homework. As outlined on page 5, every question is aligned to a language skill.

Practice pages provide instruction and assessment opportunities for each day of the school year.

Each question ties student practice to a specific language skill.

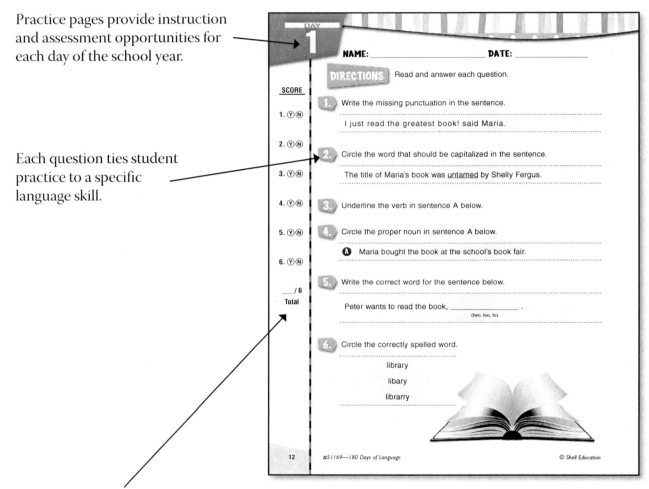

Using the Scoring Guide

Use the scoring guide along the side of each practice page to check answers and see at a glance which skills may need more reinforcement.

Fill in the appropriate circle for each problem to indicate correct (Y) or incorrect (N) responses. You might wish to indicate only incorrect responses to focus on those skills. (For example, if students consistently miss items 2 and 4, they may need additional help with those concepts as outlined in the table on page 5.) Use the answer key at the back of the book to score the problems, or you may call out answers to have students self-score or peer-score their work.

HOW TO USE THIS BOOK (cont.)

Diagnostic Assessment

Teachers can use the practice pages as diagnostic assessments. The data analysis tools included with the book enable teachers or parents to quickly score students' work and monitor their progress. Teachers and parents can see at a glance which language skills students may need to target in order to develop proficiency.

After students complete a practice page, grade each page using the answer key (pages 192–206). Then, complete the *Practice Page Item Analysis* for the appropriate day (page 8) for the whole class, or the *Student Item Analysis* (page 9) for individual students. These charts are also provided on the Digital Resource CD as PDFs, Microsoft Word® files, and as Microsoft Excel® files (filenames: pageitem.pdf, pageitem.doc, pageitem.xls; studentitem.pdf, studentitem.doc, studentitem.xls). Teachers can input data into the electronic files directly on the computer, or they can print the pages and analyze students' work using paper and pencil.

To complete the Practice Page Item Analyses:

- Write or type students' names in the far-left column. Depending on the number of students, more than one copy of the form may be needed, or you may need to add rows.

- The item numbers are included across the top of the chart. Each item correlates with the matching question number from the practice page.

- For each student, record an *X* in the column if the student has the item incorrect. If the item is correct, leave the space in the column blank.

- If you are using the Excel file, totals will be automatically generated. If you are using the Word file or if you have printed the PDF, you will need to compute the totals. Count the *X*s in each row and column and fill in the correct boxes.

To complete the Student Item Analyses:

- Write or type the student's name on the top row. This form tracks the ongoing progress of each student, so one copy per student is necessary.

- The item numbers are included across the top of the chart. Each item correlates with the matching question number from the practice page.

- For each day, record an *X* in the column if the student has the item incorrect. If the item is correct, leave the space in the column blank.

- If you are using the Excel file, totals will be automatically generated. If you are using the Word file or if you have printed the PDF, you will need to compute the totals. Count the *X*s in each row and column and fill in the correct boxes.

Practice Page Item Analysis

Directions: Record an *X* in cells to indicate where students have missed questions. Add up the totals. You can view: (1) which questions/concepts were missed per student; (2) the total correct score for each student; and (3) the total number of students who missed each question.

Day: _____ Question #	1	2	3	4	5	6	# correct
Student Name							
Sample Student		X			X	X	3/6
# of students missing each question							

HOW TO USE THIS BOOK *(cont.)*

Student Item Analysis

Directions: Record an *X* in cells to indicate where the student has missed questions. Add up the totals. You can view: (1) which questions/concepts the student missed; (2) the total correct score per day; and (3) the total number of times each question/concept was missed.

Student Name: Sample Student							
Question	**1**	**2**	**3**	**4**	**5**	**6**	**# correct**
Day							
1		X			X		4/6
Total							

HOW TO USE THIS BOOK *(cont.)*

Using the Results to Differentiate Instruction

Once results are gathered and analyzed, teachers can use the results to inform the way they differentiate instruction. The data can help determine which concepts are the most difficult for students and which need additional instructional support and continued practice. Depending on how often the practice pages are scored, results can be considered for instructional support on a daily or weekly basis.

Whole-Class Support

The results of the diagnostic analysis may show that the entire class is struggling with a particular concept or group of concepts. If these concepts have been taught in the past, this indicates that further instruction or reteaching is necessary. If these concepts have not been taught in the past, this data is a great preassessment and may demonstrate that students do not have a working knowledge of the concepts. Thus, careful planning for the length of the unit(s) or lesson(s) must be considered, and additional front-loading may be required.

Small-Group or Individual Support

The results of the diagnostic analysis may show that an individual or a small group of students is struggling with a particular concept or group of concepts. If these concepts have been taught in the past, this indicates that further instruction or reteaching is necessary. Consider pulling aside these students while others are working independently to instruct further on the concept(s). Teachers can also use the results to help identify individuals or groups of proficient students who are ready for enrichment or above-grade-level instruction. These students may benefit from independent learning contracts or more challenging activities. Students may also benefit from extra practice using games or computer-based resources.

Digital Resource CD

The Digital Resource CD provides the following resources:

- Standards Correlations Chart

- Reproducible PDFs of each practice page

- Directions for completing the diagnostic Item Analysis forms

- *Practice Page Item Analysis* PDFs, Word documents, and Excel spreadsheets

- *Student Item Analysis* PDFs, Word documents, and Excel spreadsheets

© Shell Education

STANDARDS CORRELATIONS

Shell Education is committed to producing educational materials that are research and standards based. In this effort, we have correlated all of our products to the academic standards of all 50 states, the District of Columbia, the Department of Defense Dependents Schools, and all Canadian provinces.

How to Find Standards Correlations

To print a customized correlation report of this product for your state, visit our website at http://www.shelleducation.com and follow the on-screen directions. If you require assistance in printing correlation reports, please contact our Customer Service Department at 1-877-777-3450.

Purpose and Intent of Standards

Legislation mandates that all states adopt academic standards that identify the skills students will learn in kindergarten through grade twelve. Many states also have standards for Pre–K. This same legislation sets requirements to ensure the standards are detailed and comprehensive.

Standards are designed to focus instruction and guide adoption of curricula. Standards are statements that describe the criteria necessary for students to meet specific academic goals. They define the knowledge, skills, and content students should acquire at each level. Standards are also used to develop standardized tests to evaluate students' academic progress. Teachers are required to demonstrate how their lessons meet state standards. State standards are used in the development of all of our products, so educators can be assured they meet the academic requirements of each state.

Common Core State Standards

The activities in this book are aligned to the Common Core State Standards (CCSS). The chart on page 5 lists the anchor standards. The chart is also on the Digital Resource CD (filename: standards.pdf).

NAME: _____ **DATE:** _____

DIRECTIONS Read and answer each question.

1. Ⓨ Ⓝ

2. Ⓨ Ⓝ

3. Ⓨ Ⓝ

4. Ⓨ Ⓝ

5. Ⓨ Ⓝ

6. Ⓨ Ⓝ

___ / 6
Total

1. Write the missing punctuation in the sentence.

I just read the greatest book! said Maria.

2. Circle the word that should be capitalized in the sentence.

The title of Maria's book was <u>untamed</u> by Shelly Fergus.

3. Underline the verb in sentence A below.

4. Circle the proper noun in sentence A below.

A   Maria bought the book at the school's book fair.

5. Write the correct word for the sentence below.

Peter wants to read the book, _____ .
                                         (two, too, to)

6. Circle the correctly spelled word.

library

libary

librarry

   © Shell Education

NAME: _____ **DATE:** _____

DIRECTIONS Read and answer each question.

1. Write the missing punctuation in the sentence.

Jack, Nita, and Marty ran to the bus

1. Ⓨ Ⓝ

2. Circle the word that should be capitalized in the sentence.

They always ride on the pleasantville bus at 3:30.

2. Ⓨ Ⓝ

3. Ⓨ Ⓝ

3. Underline the adverb in sentence A below.

4. Ⓨ Ⓝ

4. Circle the nouns in sentence A below.

5. Ⓨ Ⓝ

Ⓐ The friends talk happily on the bus.

6. Ⓨ Ⓝ

5. Write the correct word for the sentence.

____ / 6
Total

_____ glad they made it to the bus on time.
(Their, They're, There)

6. Circle the correctly spelled word.

anothur

an other

another

NAME: _____ **DATE:** _____

SCORE

1. Ⓨ Ⓝ

2. Ⓨ Ⓝ

3. Ⓨ Ⓝ

4. Ⓨ Ⓝ

5. Ⓨ Ⓝ

6. Ⓨ Ⓝ

___ / 6
Total

DIRECTIONS Read and answer each question.

1. Write the missing punctuation in the sentence.

Are you going to the county fair this Saturday

2. Circle the word that should be capitalized in the sentence.

mrs. Kim, Jin, and her brother are taking me.

3. Underline the pronoun in sentence A below.

4. Circle the adjective in sentence A below.

Ⓐ   I want to go on fast roller coasters.

5. Write the correct word for the sentence below.

I never want to get _____ roller coasters!
(of, off, for)

6. Circle the correctly spelled word.

amouse

amuse

aumuse

   © Shell Education

NAME: _____ **DATE:** _____

DIRECTIONS Read and answer each question.

1. Write the missing punctuation in the sentence.

Minas brother loves going to the haunted house in October.

2. Circle the word that should be capitalized in the sentence.

"Can we go there today?" mina's brother asked.

3. Underline the pronoun in sentence A below.

4. Circle the verb in sentence A below.

A They had to wait in a long line to get in.

5. Write the correct word for the sentence below.

Mina got _____ scared in the haunted house.
(quite, quit, quiet)

6. Circle the correctly spelled word.

gost

goost

ghost

1. Ⓨ Ⓝ

2. Ⓨ Ⓝ

3. Ⓨ Ⓝ

4. Ⓨ Ⓝ

5. Ⓨ Ⓝ

6. Ⓨ Ⓝ

___ / 6
Total

NAME: _____ DATE: _____

SCORE

DIRECTIONS Read and answer each question.

1. Ⓨ Ⓝ

1. Write the missing punctuation in the sentence.

Ali looked at the clock and shouted, "Im late!"

2. Ⓨ Ⓝ

2. Circle the word that should be capitalized in the sentence.

3. Ⓨ Ⓝ

hunter was waiting for Ali outside.

4. Ⓨ Ⓝ

3. Underline the plural noun in sentence A below.

4. Circle the prepositional phrase in sentence A below.

5. Ⓨ Ⓝ

Ⓐ "Let's ride our bikes to the zoo," Ali said.

6. Ⓨ Ⓝ

5. Write the correct word for the sentence below.

___ / 6
Total

" _____ animals do you want to see first?" Ali asked.
(Witch, Which, Where)

6. Circle the correctly spelled word.

duaghter

daughter

daughtur

© Shell Education

NAME: _____ **DATE:** _____

DIRECTIONS Read and answer each question.

1. Write the missing punctuation in the sentence.

"Would you like to go to the animal rescue " Mila asked Raisa.

1. Y N

2. Circle the word that should be capitalized in the sentence.

Let's go to the store on main Street.

2. Y N

3. Y N

3. Underline the proper nouns in sentence A below.

4. Y N

4. Circle the verb in sentence A below.

5. Y N

A Mila and Raisa stopped at noon for a snack.

6. Y N

5. Write the correct word for the sentence below.

____ / 6
Total

"What would happen if a rabbit got _____?" Raisa wondered.
(lose, louse, loose)

6. Circle the correctly spelled word.

raccoon

racoon

raccune

NAME: _____ **DATE:** _____

SCORE

1. Ⓨ Ⓝ

2. Ⓨ Ⓝ

3. Ⓨ Ⓝ

4. Ⓨ Ⓝ

5. Ⓨ Ⓝ

6. Ⓨ Ⓝ

___ / 6
Total

DIRECTIONS Read and answer each question.

1. Write the missing punctuation in the sentence.

Ethan's favorite places are rivers lakes, and creeks.

2. Circle the words that should be capitalized in the sentence.

Lyla and Ethan had a snack by sand hill River.

3. Underline the preposition in sentence A below.

4. Circle the pronoun in sentence A below.

Ⓐ It was cooler sitting by the river.

5. Write the correct word for the sentence below.

The wind was blowing _____ the trees.
(throe, though, through)

6. Circle the correctly spelled word.

skratch

scratch

scracth

© Shell Education

NAME: _____ **DATE:** _____

DIRECTIONS Read and answer each question.

1. Write the missing punctuation in the sentence.

Owen said, "I'm getting tired. I think it's time to go home.

1. Ⓨ Ⓝ

2. Circle the word that should be capitalized in the sentence.

cole said, "Maybe my dad can pick us up."

2. Ⓨ Ⓝ

3. Ⓨ Ⓝ

3. Underline the conjunction in sentence A below.

4. Ⓨ Ⓝ

4. Circle the verb in sentence A below.

5. Ⓨ Ⓝ

Ⓐ   Cole and Owen waited tiredly by their bikes.

6. Ⓨ Ⓝ

5. Write the correct word for the sentence below.

___ / 6
Total

Both of _____ parents came to get them.
         (they're, there, their)

6. Circle the correctly spelled word.

luckely

luckily

lukily

NAME: _____ **DATE:** _____

SCORE

1. Y N

2. Y N

3. Y N

4. Y N

5. Y N

6. Y N

___ / 6
Total

DIRECTIONS Read and answer each question.

1. Write the missing punctuation in the sentence.

Shall we pick up a pizza for dinner tonight?" Riku's dad asked.

2. Circle the word that should be capitalized in the sentence.

"That would be great, mr. Sato," Sami replied.

3. Underline the adjectives in sentence A below.

4. Circle the adverb in sentence A below.

A They waited hungrily for a large pizza.

5. Write the correct word for the sentence below.

The _____ of pizza filled the car as they drove home.
(sent, cent, scent)

6. Circle the correctly spelled word.

greatful

grateful

greetful

NAME: _____ **DATE:** _____

DIRECTIONS Read and answer each question.

SCORE

1. Write the missing punctuation in the sentence.

"What shall we do tomorrow " Kala asked.

1. Ⓨ Ⓝ

2. Circle the word that should be capitalized in the sentence.

"It's hard to think about that when i'm this tired," said Dominic.

2. Ⓨ Ⓝ

3. Ⓨ Ⓝ

3. Underline the proper noun in sentence A below.

4. Ⓨ Ⓝ

4. Circle the pronoun in sentence A below.

5. Ⓨ Ⓝ

Ⓐ "You just need some sleep," said Dad.

6. Ⓨ Ⓝ

5. Write the correct word for the sentence below.

"I think you're right," Dominic _____.
(side, sighed, sided)

___ / 6
Total

6. Circle the correctly spelled word.

paeceful

peaceful

pieceful

© Shell Education

NAME: _____   **DATE:** _____

SCORE

DIRECTIONS Read and answer each question.

1. Ⓨ Ⓝ

1. Write the missing punctuation in the sentence.

Yuki read a book about Susan B Anthony.

2. Ⓨ Ⓝ

2. Circle the word that should be capitalized in the sentence.

3. Ⓨ Ⓝ

She was the first woman to have her picture on an american coin.

4. Ⓨ Ⓝ

3. Underline the verb in sentence A below.

5. Ⓨ Ⓝ

4. Circle the prepositional phrase in sentence A below.

Ⓐ Ms. Anthony fought for women's rights.

6. Ⓨ Ⓝ

5. Write the correct word for the sentence below.

____ / 6
Total

She _____ how to work for change.
(new, knew, gnu)

6. Circle the correctly spelled word.

ability

abillity

ubility

                    © Shell Education

NAME: _____ **DATE:** _____

DIRECTIONS Read and answer each question.

1. Write the missing punctuation in the sentence.

Amin likes to read books about writers

1. Ⓨ Ⓝ

2. Circle the word that should be capitalized in the sentence.

He read a book about Louisa may Alcott.

2. Ⓨ Ⓝ

3. Ⓨ Ⓝ

3. Circle the adjectives in sentence A below.

4. Ⓨ Ⓝ

4. Underline the pronoun in sentence A below.

5. Ⓨ Ⓝ

Ⓐ Her most famous book was <u>Little Women</u>.

6. Ⓨ Ⓝ

5. Write the correct word for the sentence below.

___ / 6
Total

Amin would love to _____ a writer someday.
(meat, meet, mete)

6. Circle the correctly spelled word.

authur

author

auther

NAME: _____   **DATE:** _____

SCORE

1. Y N

2. Y N

3. Y N

4. Y N

5. Y N

6. Y N

___ / 6
Total

DIRECTIONS Read and answer each question.

1. Write the missing punctuation in the sentence.

A famous ocean liner sank on April 15 1912.

2. Circle the word that should be capitalized in the sentence.

It was named the RMS *titanic.*

3. Underline the nouns in sentence A below.

4. Circle the verbs in sentence A below.

A The ship struck an iceberg and sank in the icy water.

5. Write the correct word for the sentence below.

Not having enough lifeboats was the _____ problem.
(Maine, mane, main)

6. Circle the correctly spelled word.

beneeth

beeneath

beneath

   © Shell Education

NAME: _____ **DATE:** _____

DIRECTIONS Read and answer each question.

1. Write the missing punctuation in the sentence.

Do you have a bicycle

1. Ⓨ Ⓝ

2. Circle the word that should be capitalized in the sentence.

The Schwinn bicycle Company was founded in 1895.

2. Ⓨ Ⓝ

3. Ⓨ Ⓝ

3. Underline the verb in sentence A below.

4. Ⓨ Ⓝ

4. Circle the preposition in sentence A below.

5. Ⓨ Ⓝ

Ⓐ The factories produced a million bikes in the year 1900.

6. Ⓨ Ⓝ

5. Write the correct word for the sentence below.

___ / 6
Total

Each bike _____ about 20 pounds (9 kilograms) in 1900.

(wade, weighed, weight)

6. Circle the correctly spelled word.

ferther

further

firther

NAME: _____ **DATE:** _____

SCORE

1. Ⓨ Ⓝ

2. Ⓨ Ⓝ

3. Ⓨ Ⓝ

4. Ⓨ Ⓝ

5. Ⓨ Ⓝ

6. Ⓨ Ⓝ

___ / 6
Total

DIRECTIONS Read and answer each question.

1. Write the missing punctuation in the sentence.

Would you like to travel on a train a ship, or a plane?

2. Circle the word that should be capitalized in the sentence.

You can travel on any of them from San francisco.

3. Underline the proper noun in sentence A below.

4. Circle the verb in sentence A below.

A San Francisco is usually chilly.

5. Write the correct word for the sentence below.

The _____ is often foggy in San Francisco.
(weather, whether, wetter)

6. Circle the correctly spelled word.

purpose

perpose

porpose

© Shell Education

NAME: _____ **DATE:** _____

SCORE

DIRECTIONS Read and answer each question.

1. Write the missing punctuation in the sentence.

Neo likes to swim and Ellie likes to ride bikes.

1. Ⓨ Ⓝ

2. Circle the word that should be capitalized in the sentence.

They decided to bike to the oakdale swimming pool.

2. Ⓨ Ⓝ

3. Ⓨ Ⓝ

3. Underline the common nouns in sentence A below.

4. Ⓨ Ⓝ

4. Circle the preposition in sentence A below.

5. Ⓨ Ⓝ

Ⓐ Neo and Ellie tied ribbons on their bikes.

6. Ⓨ Ⓝ

5. Write the correct word for the sentence below.

___ / 6

Neo and Ellie got their bikes on _____.

(sail, sale)

Total

6. Circle the correctly spelled word.

persude

persaude

persuade

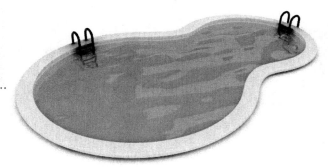

NAME: _____ **DATE:** _____

SCORE

DIRECTIONS Read and answer each question.

1. (Y)(N)

1. Write the missing punctuation in the sentence.

....

Have you been to New York City New York?

....

2. (Y)(N)

2. Circle the word that should be capitalized in the sentence.

....

3. (Y)(N)

Some people think it is the most exciting city in the united States.

....

4. (Y)(N)

3. Underline the pronoun in sentence A below.

4. Circle the proper noun in sentence A below.

5. (Y)(N)

....

A You can see shows on Broadway or go to museums.

....

6. (Y)(N)

5. Write the correct word for the sentence below.

....

___ / 6

Total

_____ is lots to do in New York City.

(Their, They're, There)

....

6. Circle the correctly spelled word.

....

populer

popular

populare

#51169—180 Days of Language

© Shell Education

NAME: _____ **DATE:** _____

DIRECTIONS Read and answer each question.

1. Write the missing punctuation in the sentence.

What is your favorite city

2. Circle the word that should be capitalized in the sentence.

Is it in the united States or another country?

3. Underline the verb in sentence A below.

4. Circle the complete subject in sentence A below.

A Many people like home most of all.

5. Write the correct word for the sentence below.

Maybe _____ favorite city is far away.

(you're, your)

6. Circle the correctly spelled word.

seeze

sieze

seize

1. Ⓨ Ⓝ

2. Ⓨ Ⓝ

3. Ⓨ Ⓝ

4. Ⓨ Ⓝ

5. Ⓨ Ⓝ

6. Ⓨ Ⓝ

___ / 6
Total

NAME: _____ **DATE:** _____

SCORE

1. Ⓨ Ⓝ

2. Ⓨ Ⓝ

3. Ⓨ Ⓝ

4. Ⓨ Ⓝ

5. Ⓨ Ⓝ

6. Ⓨ Ⓝ

____ / 6
Total

DIRECTIONS Read and answer each question.

1. Write the missing punctuation in the sentence.

The first snowboard was invented in Muskegon Michigan.

2. Circle the word that should be capitalized in the sentence.

It was invented by sherman Poppen.

3. Underline the proper noun in sentence A below.

4. Circle the conjunction in sentence A below.

Ⓐ He tied two skis together and called it a *Snurfer*.

5. Write the correct word for the sentence below.

Snowboarding would be fun for _____ to try.
(ewe, you, yew)

6. Circle the correctly spelled word.

slippery

slipery

slipperry

 © Shell Education

NAME: _____ **DATE:** _____

DIRECTIONS Read and answer each question.

SCORE

1. Write the missing punctuation in the sentence.

What did you have for dinner last night

1. Ⓨ Ⓝ

2. Circle the word that should be capitalized in the sentence.

Roi's favorite restaurant is Big Joe's diner.

2. Ⓨ Ⓝ

3. Ⓨ Ⓝ

3. Underline the verb in sentence A below.

4. Ⓨ Ⓝ

4. Circle the proper noun in sentence A below.

Ⓐ Roi always orders french toast.

5. Ⓨ Ⓝ

6. Ⓨ Ⓝ

5. Write the correct word for the sentence below.

_____ always hot and tasty.
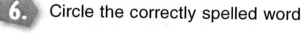
(There, Their, They're)

___ / 6
Total

6. Circle the correctly spelled word.

spoled

spoilled

spoiled

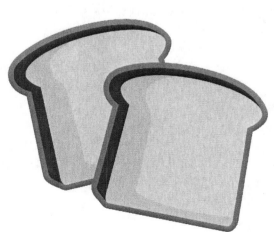

NAME: _____ DATE: _____

DIRECTIONS Read and answer each question.

SCORE

1. Ⓨ Ⓝ

2. Ⓨ Ⓝ

3. Ⓨ Ⓝ

4. Ⓨ Ⓝ

5. Ⓨ Ⓝ

6. Ⓨ Ⓝ

___ / 6
Total

1. Write the missing punctuation in the sentence.

Jasmines best friend is Morgan

2. Circle the words that should be capitalized in the sentence.

They love to watch the *star wars* movies.

3. Underline the verb in sentence A below.

4. Circle the pronoun in sentence A below.

Ⓐ   Jasmine took Morgan to the movies for her birthday.

5. Write the correct word for the sentence below.

_____ even better to have popcorn at the movies!
(Its, It's, It)

6. Circle the correctly spelled word.

beleivable

believable

believible

   © Shell Education

NAME: _____ **DATE:** _____

DIRECTIONS Read and answer each question.

1. Write the missing punctuation in the sentence.

"Stop, thief " cried the giant to Jack.

1. Ⓨ Ⓝ

2. Ⓨ Ⓝ

2. Circle the word that should be capitalized in the sentence.

But jack hung onto the harp and climbed down the beanstalk.

3. Ⓨ Ⓝ

3. Underline the adjectives in sentence A below.

4. Ⓨ Ⓝ

4. Circle the pronoun in sentence A below.

5. Ⓨ Ⓝ

Ⓐ He chopped at the huge beanstalk.

6. Ⓨ Ⓝ

5. Write the correct word for the sentence below.

___ / 6
Total

The giant couldn't _____ down fast enough.
(clime, clim, climb)

6. Circle the correctly spelled word.

haevy

hevvy

heavy

NAME: _____ **DATE:** _____

SCORE

1. Ⓨ Ⓝ

2. Ⓨ Ⓝ

3. Ⓨ Ⓝ

4. Ⓨ Ⓝ

5. Ⓨ Ⓝ

6. Ⓨ Ⓝ

___ / 6
Total

DIRECTIONS Read and answer each question.

1. Write the missing punctuation in the sentence.

When she was young, my mothers favorite book was <u>Peter Pan</u>.

2. Circle the word that should be capitalized in the sentence.

<u>Peter Pan</u> was written by J. M. barrie.

3. Underline the verb in sentence A below.

4. Circle the proper noun in sentence A below.

Ⓐ Tinker Bell resembles a tinkling bell.

5. Write the correct word for the sentence below.

Tinker Bell was a _____.
(ferry, fairy, farely)

6. Circle the correctly spelled word.

magical

magiccal

majical

© Shell Education

NAME: _____ **DATE:** _____

DIRECTIONS Read and answer each question.

1. Write the missing punctuation in the sentence.

"Let's take out the sailboat at 2 00 P.M.," Finn said.

1. Ⓨ Ⓝ

2. Circle the word that should be capitalized in the sentence.

Finn's sailboat is called the *sharkfin*.

2. Ⓨ Ⓝ

3. Ⓨ Ⓝ

3. Underline the verb in sentence A below.

4. Ⓨ Ⓝ

4. Circle the adjective in sentence A below.

5. Ⓨ Ⓝ

Ⓐ Finn likes sailing on beautiful Lake Louise.

6. Ⓨ Ⓝ

5. Write the correct word for the sentence below.

Someday, he'd like to sail the seven _____.

(sees, sea, seas)

___ / 6
Total

6. Circle the correctly spelled word.

harbir

harbor

harbur

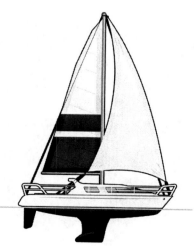

NAME: _____ DATE: _____

DIRECTIONS Read and answer each question.

1. Ⓨ Ⓝ

2. Ⓨ Ⓝ

3. Ⓨ Ⓝ

4. Ⓨ Ⓝ

5. Ⓨ Ⓝ

6. Ⓨ Ⓝ

___ / 6
Total

1. Write the missing punctuation in the sentence.

African elephants can be found in Kenya Africa.

2. Circle the word that should be capitalized in the sentence.

They can also be found in south Africa.

3. Underline the plural nouns in sentence A below.

4. Circle the conjunction in sentence A below.

Ⓐ You can see elephants and other animals on a safari.

5. Write the correct word for the sentence below.

Sometimes, other animals _____ on the elephants.
(prey, pray)

6. Circle the correctly spelled word.

weigh

wiegh

weagh

NAME: _____ **DATE:** _____

SCORE

1. Write the missing punctuation in the sentence.

1. Ⓨ Ⓝ

Some people live in houses and some people live in condos.

2. Circle the word that should be capitalized in the sentence.

2. Ⓨ Ⓝ

There's an apartment building in New York City on Spruce street.

3. Ⓨ Ⓝ

3. Underline the pronoun in sentence A below.

4. Ⓨ Ⓝ

4. Circle the preposition in sentence A below.

5. Ⓨ Ⓝ

Ⓐ Would you live 76 floors above the ground?

6. Ⓨ Ⓝ

5. Write the correct word for the sentence below.

___ / 6
Total

You could _____ at the amazing views.
(stair, stare, start)

6. Circle the correctly spelled word.

firniture

furniture

funiture

NAME: _____ DATE: _____

DIRECTIONS Read and answer each question.

1. Write the missing punctuation in the sentence.

1. Ⓨ Ⓝ

Years ago people did most of their cooking over fires.

2. Ⓨ Ⓝ

2. Circle the word that should be capitalized in the sentence.

3. Ⓨ Ⓝ

You can still cook over a fire at Morris State park.

4. Ⓨ Ⓝ

3. Underline the pronoun in sentence A below.

5. Ⓨ Ⓝ

4. Circle the adjective in sentence A below.

Ⓐ However, you must use the black pits.

6. Ⓨ Ⓝ

5. Write the correct word for the sentence below.

___ / 6
Total

You _____ not want to start a forest fire!
        (would, wood)

6. Circle the correctly spelled word.

nives

knifs

knives

    © Shell Education

NAME: _____ **DATE:** _____

DIRECTIONS Read and answer each question.

1. Write the missing punctuation in the sentence.

Let's go to see the parade tomorrow," said Elijah.

1. Ⓨ Ⓝ

2. Circle the word that should be capitalized in the sentence.

The parade starts at river Steet Park.

2. Ⓨ Ⓝ

3. Ⓨ Ⓝ

3. Underline the proper noun in sentence A below.

4. Ⓨ Ⓝ

4. Circle the adjectives in sentence A below.

5. Ⓨ Ⓝ

A Elijah thinks decorative floats are the best part of the parade.

6. Ⓨ Ⓝ

5. Write the correct word for the sentence below.

___ / 6
Total

The parade will be held _____ it is rainy or sunny.
(weather, whether)

6. Circle the correctly spelled word.

neighbor

neaghbor

nieghbor

NAME: _____ **DATE:** _____

DIRECTIONS Read and answer each question.

1. ⓎⓃ

1. Write the missing punctuation in the sentence.

....

Many art museums have artwork by Claude Monet

....

2. ⓎⓃ

2. Circle the word that should be capitalized in the sentence.

....

3. ⓎⓃ

Monet was born in paris, France, in 1840.

....

4. ⓎⓃ

3. Underline the verbs in sentence A below.

5. ⓎⓃ

4. Circle the preposition in sentence A below.

....

Ⓐ He painted in new ways, using light brushstrokes.

6. ⓎⓃ

....

5. Write the correct word for the sentence below.

....

___ / 6
Total

Impressionism became a popular _____of art.
(style, stile, styles)

....

6. Circle the correctly spelled word.

....

flower

flowr

flouwer

....

   © Shell Education

NAME: _____ **DATE:** _____

> **DIRECTIONS** Read and answer each question.

1. Write the missing punctuation in the sentence.

Have you ever seen a Maine Coon cat

2. Circle the word that should be capitalized in the sentence.

Some people think Captain charles Coon brought these cats to America.

3. Underline the adjectives in sentence A below.

4. Circle the nouns in sentence A below.

A Others think these long-haired cats are related to raccoons.

5. Write the correct word for the sentence below.

The _____ feature of this cat is its size. It's big!
(main, Maine, mane)

6. Circle the correctly spelled word.

loyle

loial

loyal

1. Ⓨ Ⓝ
2. Ⓨ Ⓝ
3. Ⓨ Ⓝ
4. Ⓨ Ⓝ
5. Ⓨ Ⓝ
6. Ⓨ Ⓝ

___ / 6
Total

NAME: _____ DATE: _____

DIRECTIONS Read and answer each question.

1. Ⓨ Ⓝ

2. Ⓨ Ⓝ

3. Ⓨ Ⓝ

4. Ⓨ Ⓝ

5. Ⓨ Ⓝ

6. Ⓨ Ⓝ

___ / 6
Total

1. Write the missing punctuation in the sentence.

Would you like to get paid for taking a walk

2. Circle the word that should be capitalized in the sentence.

Teens who work at the Dog walk Company do!

3. Underline the preposition in sentence A below.

4. Circle the pronoun in sentence A below.

Ⓐ They walk four dogs in a group.

5. Write the correct word for the sentence below.

Dog walking _____ the best job for you someday!
(may be, maybe)

6. Circle the correctly spelled word.

beste

beast

beest

NAME: _____ **DATE:** _____

DIRECTIONS Read and answer each question.

1. Write the missing punctuation in the sentence.

Your mouth includes a tongue, a roof, a base, teeth, and lips

1. Ⓨ Ⓝ

2. Circle the word that should be capitalized in the sentence.

Dr. perez is an orthodontist in the city.

2. Ⓨ Ⓝ

3. Ⓨ Ⓝ

3. Underline the possessive pronoun in sentence A below.

4. Ⓨ Ⓝ

4. Circle the verb in sentence A below.

Ⓐ An orthodontist made my teeth straight.

5. Ⓨ Ⓝ

6. Ⓨ Ⓝ

5. Write the correct word for the sentence below.

Would you like to _____ into mouths all day?
(pear, peer, pier)

___ / 6
Total

6. Circle the correctly spelled word.

swallow

swalow

swolow

NAME: _____ DATE: _____

DIRECTIONS Read and answer each question.

1. Ⓨ Ⓝ

1. Write the missing punctuation in the sentence.

The Gateway Arch is in St. Louis Missouri.

2. Ⓨ Ⓝ

2. Circle the word that should be capitalized in the sentence.

3. Ⓨ Ⓝ

The capital of Missouri is Jefferson city.

4. Ⓨ Ⓝ

3. Underline the common nouns in sentence A below.

5. Ⓨ Ⓝ

4. Circle the proper nouns in sentence A below.

Ⓐ Kira and Lina like to take the train to the city.

6. Ⓨ Ⓝ

5. Write the correct word for the sentence below.

___ / 6
Total

Kira and Lina like to shop the _____ in the city.
(sails, sales)

6. Circle the correctly spelled word.

guvenor

govenor

governor

NAME: _____ **DATE:** _____

DIRECTIONS Read and answer each question.

1. Write the missing punctuation in the sentence.

Watch out for the car

1. Ⓨ Ⓝ

2. Circle the words that should be capitalized in the sentence.

henry ford first produced the popular ford Model T car in 1908.

2. Ⓨ Ⓝ

3. Ⓨ Ⓝ

3. Underline the adjective in sentence A below.

4. Ⓨ Ⓝ

4. Circle the common noun in sentence A below.

5. Ⓨ Ⓝ

Ⓐ Ford produced affordable cars.

6. Ⓨ Ⓝ

5. Write the correct word for the sentence below.

___ / 6
Total

The prices were so low that lots of people could _____ them.
(by, buy)

6. Circle the correctly spelled word.

causion

cawtion

caution

NAME: _____ DATE: _____

DIRECTIONS Read and answer each question.

1. (Y)(N)

2. (Y)(N)

3. (Y)(N)

4. (Y)(N)

5. (Y)(N)

6. (Y)(N)

___ / 6
Total

1. Write the missing punctuation in the sentence.

....

Bo fetch the stick!

....

2. Circle the word that should be capitalized in the sentence.

....

Bo loves to play fetch with jaden.

....

3. Underline the proper nouns in sentence A below.

4. Circle the adjectives in sentence A below.

....

A Bo is a huge sheepdog from Australia.

....

5. Write the correct word for the sentence below.

....

Sheepdogs like to work and play _____ hard.
(vary, very, varied)

....

6. Circle the correctly spelled word.

....

wurried

worried

worryed

....

© Shell Education

NAME: _____ **DATE:** _____

DIRECTIONS Read and answer each question.

1. Write the missing punctuation in the sentence.

"Lets go see the sharks at the aquarium," Laila said.

1. Ⓨ Ⓝ

2. Circle the word that should be capitalized in the sentence.

The Monterey aquarium has a great white shark in a tank.

2. Ⓨ Ⓝ

3. Ⓨ Ⓝ

3. Underline the verb in sentence A below.

4. Ⓨ Ⓝ

4. Circle the adjectives in sentence A below.

Ⓐ Sharks eat sea lions, bony fish, and other sharks.

5. Ⓨ Ⓝ

6. Ⓨ Ⓝ

5. Write the correct word for the sentence below.

You could say that great white sharks _____ over the
ocean like kings.   (rain, reign, rein)

___ / 6
Total

6. Circle the correctly spelled word.

huried

hirried

hurried

NAME: _____ DATE: _____

Read and answer each question.

SCORE

1. Ⓨ Ⓝ

2. Ⓨ Ⓝ

3. Ⓨ Ⓝ

4. Ⓨ Ⓝ

5. Ⓨ Ⓝ

6. Ⓨ Ⓝ

___ / 6
Total

1. Write the missing punctuation in the sentence.

Rio wanted to go on a treasure hunt but Mai wanted to play inside.

2. Circle the word that should be capitalized in the sentence.

"Let's pretend I'm blackbeard," Rio said.

3. Underline the preposition in sentence A below.

4. Circle the article in sentence A below.

Ⓐ Mai had read about a female pirate named Anne Bonny.

5. Write the correct word for the sentence below.

Women pirates dressed like men to seek _____ fortune.

(there, their, they're)

6. Circle the correctly spelled word.

disagree

disagrea

disargee

NAME: _____ DATE: _____

DAY
38

DIRECTIONS Read and answer each question.

SCORE

1. Write the missing punctuation in the sentence.

The Abraham Lincoln Presidential Library is in Springfield Illinois.

1. Ⓨ Ⓝ

2. Circle the word that should be capitalized in the sentence.

Springfield is near Clear lake.

2. Ⓨ Ⓝ

3. Ⓨ Ⓝ

3. Underline the verb in sentence A below.

4. Ⓨ Ⓝ

4. Circle the proper nouns in sentence A below.

Ⓐ Springfield is smaller than Chicago.

5. Ⓨ Ⓝ

6. Ⓨ Ⓝ

5. Write the correct word for the sentence below.

Springfield would be a good city for _____ vacation.
(your, yore, you're)

___ / 6
Total

6. Circle the correctly spelled word.

surface

surfice

sirface

© Shell Education

#51169—180 Days of Language

49

NAME: _____ DATE: _____

DIRECTIONS Read and answer each question.

1. Ⓨ Ⓝ

2. Ⓨ Ⓝ

3. Ⓨ Ⓝ

4. Ⓨ Ⓝ

5. Ⓨ Ⓝ

6. Ⓨ Ⓝ

___ / 6
Total

1. Write the missing punctuation in the sentence.

Would you like to go on an ocean liner

2. Circle the word that should be capitalized in the sentence.

One very long cruise ship is called the *Oasis of the seas*.

3. Underline the verb in sentence A below.

4. Circle the preposition in sentence A below.

Ⓐ More than 2,000 people work on the ship.

5. Write the correct word for the sentence below.

A ship that big _____ a lot!
(ways, weigh, weighs)

6. Circle the correctly spelled word.

starecase

staircase

staircais

© Shell Education

NAME: _____ **DATE:** _____

DIRECTIONS Read and answer each question.

1. Write the missing punctuation in the sentence.

....

Have you visited our nation's capital city

1. Ⓨ Ⓝ

2. Circle the word that should be capitalized in the sentence.

....

Washington, D.C., is on the Potomac river.

2. Ⓨ Ⓝ

3. Ⓨ Ⓝ

3. Underline the plural noun in sentence A below.

4. Ⓨ Ⓝ

4. Circle the proper noun in sentence A below.

....

Ⓐ You can visit many museums and see the Capitol.

5. Ⓨ Ⓝ

6. Ⓨ Ⓝ

5. Write the correct word for the sentence below.

....

You won't forget the _____ of the monuments at night.
(sight, cite, site)

....

___ / 6
Total

6. Circle the correctly spelled word.

....

preserve

perserve

presserve

NAME: _____ DATE: _____

SCORE

1. Ⓨ Ⓝ

2. Ⓨ Ⓝ

3. Ⓨ Ⓝ

4. Ⓨ Ⓝ

5. Ⓨ Ⓝ

6. Ⓨ Ⓝ

___ / 6
Total

DIRECTIONS Read and answer each question.

1. Write the missing punctuation in the sentence.

"Clang, clang, clang " went the trolley.

2. Circle the word that should be capitalized in the sentence.

Those are words from "The trolley Song."

3. Underline the prepositions in sentence A below.

4. Circle the proper nouns in sentence A below.

Ⓐ Judy Garland sang the song in a movie called *Meet Me in St. Louis.*

5. Write the correct word for the sentence below.

She was _____ famous for her singing.
                (quite, quiet, quit)

6. Circle the correctly spelled word.

purform

perrform

perform

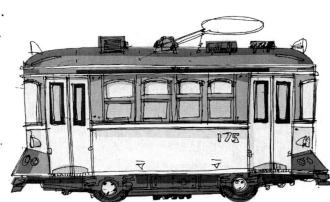

NAME: _____ **DATE:** _____

DIRECTIONS Read and answer each question.

SCORE

1. Write the missing punctuation in the sentence.

The Air Force Academy is in Colorado Springs Colorado.

1. Ⓨ Ⓝ

2. Circle the words that should be capitalized in the sentence.

Students are members of the air force.

2. Ⓨ Ⓝ

3. Ⓨ Ⓝ

3. Underline the conjunction in sentence A below.

4. Ⓨ Ⓝ

4. Circle the complete subject in sentence A below.

5. Ⓨ Ⓝ

Ⓐ Students attend college classes and learn to fly.

6. Ⓨ Ⓝ

5. Write the correct word for the sentence below.

Students not only study hard, but they learn to be leaders,

_____.

(to, too, two)

___ / 6
Total

6. Circle the correctly spelled word.

general

generul

genaral

NAME: _____ DATE: _____

DIRECTIONS Read and answer each question.

1. Ⓨ Ⓝ

2. Ⓨ Ⓝ

3. Ⓨ Ⓝ

4. Ⓨ Ⓝ

5. Ⓨ Ⓝ

6. Ⓨ Ⓝ

___ / 6
Total

1. Write the missing punctuation in the sentence.

The *Viking 1* spacecraft was launched on August 20 1975.

2. Circle the word that should be capitalized in the sentence.

The spacecraft took eleven months to get to mars.

3. Underline the verb in sentence A below.

4. Circle the article in sentence A below.

Ⓐ The spacecraft searched for signs of life.

5. Write the correct word for the sentence below.

Maybe someday, a _____ will land on Mars!
(humane, human)

6. Circle the correctly spelled word.

voyuge

voiyage

voyage

© Shell Education

NAME: _____ **DATE:** _____

DIRECTIONS Read and answer each question.

1. Write the missing punctuation in the sentence.

Have you ever visited a cemetery

1. Ⓨ Ⓝ

2. Circle the word that should be capitalized in the sentence.

Boothill Graveyard is in tombstone, Arizona.

2. Ⓨ Ⓝ

3. Ⓨ Ⓝ

3. Underline the adjective that describes the subject in sentence A below.

4. Ⓨ Ⓝ

4. Circle the helping verb in sentence A below.

Ⓐ Many people were buried in the 1880s.

5. Ⓨ Ⓝ

6. Ⓨ Ⓝ

5. Write the correct word for the sentence below.

The town is known _____ burying the first pioneers.
          (for, fore, four)

___ / 6
Total

6. Circle the correctly spelled word.

countrys

countries

countris

RIP

NAME: _____ **DATE:** _____

SCORE

1. Ⓨ Ⓝ

2. Ⓨ Ⓝ

3. Ⓨ Ⓝ

4. Ⓨ Ⓝ

5. Ⓨ Ⓝ

6. Ⓨ Ⓝ

___ / 6
Total

DIRECTIONS Read and answer each question.

1. Write the missing punctuation in the sentence.

If you drive in New England you might go on a famous road.

2. Circle the word that should be capitalized in the sentence.

The Boston post Road began as trails before the colonists came.

3. Underline the contraction in sentence A below.

4. Circle the conjunction in sentence A below.

A It's also called the Post Road or the Boston Road.

5. Write the correct word for the sentence below.

The _____ takes drivers from New York City to Boston.
(route, root, rote)

6. Circle the correctly spelled word.

private

privite

privute

NAME: _____ **DATE:** _____

| DIRECTIONS | Read and answer each question. |

SCORE

1. Write the missing punctuation in the sentence.

Beijing China, is the biggest city in the world.

1. Ⓨ Ⓝ

2. Circle the word that should be capitalized in the sentence.

Beijing used to be called peking.

2. Ⓨ Ⓝ

3. Ⓨ Ⓝ

3. Underline the complete subject in sentence A below.

4. Ⓨ Ⓝ

4. Circle the verb in sentence A below.

Ⓐ Many Beijing visitors tour the nearby Great Wall.

5. Ⓨ Ⓝ

6. Ⓨ Ⓝ

5. Write the correct word for the sentence below.

___ / 6
Total

You can see far _____ in the distance from the top of the Great Wall.   (off, of)

6. Circle the correctly spelled word.

bridje

brige

bridge

NAME: _____ DATE: _____

DIRECTIONS Read and answer each question.

1. Ⓨ Ⓝ

2. Ⓨ Ⓝ

3. Ⓨ Ⓝ

4. Ⓨ Ⓝ

5. Ⓨ Ⓝ

6. Ⓨ Ⓝ

___ / 6
Total

1. Write the missing punctuation in the sentence.

If you lived years ago your chewing gum came from a tree.

2. Circle the word that should be capitalized in the sentence.

american Indians peeled off the bark and scraped off the sticky part.

3. Underline the helping verb in sentence A below.

4. Circle the conjunction in sentence A below.

Ⓐ   Resin, the gum, was used in medicine and chewing gum.

5. Write the correct word for the sentence below.

When you _____ your gum, think about the sweet-gum
tree!   (chews, choose, chose)

6. Circle the correctly spelled word.

smoth

smooth

smouth

© Shell Education

NAME: _____ **DATE:** _____

DIRECTIONS Read and answer each question.

1. Write the missing punctuation in the sentence.

Did you know that you can erase with a dry crust of bread

1. Ⓨ Ⓝ

2. Circle the word that should be capitalized in the sentence.

Edward naime picked up some rubber by mistake and began erasing.

2. Ⓨ Ⓝ

3. Ⓨ Ⓝ

3. Underline the pronoun in sentence A below.

4. Ⓨ Ⓝ

4. Circle the verbs in sentence A below.

5. Ⓨ Ⓝ

Ⓐ He discovered that rubber worked better than bread!

6. Ⓨ Ⓝ

5. Write the correct word for the sentence below.

___ / 6
Total

He began to _____ squares of rubber for erasing.
(cell, sell, sale)

6. Circle the correctly spelled word.

acheeve

acheive

achieve

NAME: _____ DATE: _____

DIRECTIONS Read and answer each question.

1. (Y) (N)

2. (Y) (N)

3. (Y) (N)

4. (Y) (N)

5. (Y) (N)

6. (Y) (N)

___ / 6
Total

1. Write the missing punctuation in the sentence.

....

Coltons favorite sport is football.

....

2. Circle the word that should be capitalized in the sentence.

....

He dreams of playing for the Denver broncos when he grows up.

....

3. Underline the adjective in sentence A below.

4. Circle the proper noun in sentence A below.

....

A Colton likes kicking field goals.

....

5. Write the correct word for the sentence below.

....

It's a _____ to grab another player's helmet.
           (fowl, foul)

....

6. Circle the correctly spelled word.

....

guard

gaurd

gard

NAME: _____ **DATE:** _____

DIRECTIONS Read and answer each question.

SCORE

1. Write the missing punctuation in the sentence.

There is nothing better than a clear autumn day

1. Ⓨ Ⓝ

2. Circle the word that should be capitalized in the sentence.

The best time to look at colorful leaves is in october.

2. Ⓨ Ⓝ

3. Ⓨ Ⓝ

3. Underline the pronoun in sentence A below.

4. Ⓨ Ⓝ

4. Circle the adjectives in sentence A below.

Ⓐ We go on long drives during fall to see the leaves.

5. Ⓨ Ⓝ

6. Ⓨ Ⓝ

5. Write the correct word for the sentence below.

I also like to walk _____ piles of leaves.
(through, threw, throw)

___ / 6
Total

6. Circle the correctly spelled word.

stedy

steady

steedy

NAME: _____ **DATE:** _____

SCORE

1. Ⓨ Ⓝ

2. Ⓨ Ⓝ

3. Ⓨ Ⓝ

4. Ⓨ Ⓝ

5. Ⓨ Ⓝ

6. Ⓨ Ⓝ

___ / 6
Total

DIRECTIONS Read and answer each question.

1. Write the missing punctuation in the sentence.

Its been more than 100 years since the ballpoint pen was invented.

2. Circle the word that should be capitalized in the sentence.

Laszlo biro, a journalist, noticed how newspaper ink dried quickly.

3. Underline the linking verb in sentence A below.

4. Circle the article in sentence A below.

Ⓐ Newspaper ink was too thick for a fountain pen.

5. Write the correct word for the sentence below.

He put a ball in the pen, which picked up the ink. It was _____.

(prefect, perfect)

6. Circle the correctly spelled word.

relief

releef

releaf

NAME: _____ **DATE:** _____

DIRECTIONS Read and answer each question.

SCORE

1. Write the missing punctuation in the sentence.

Nita begins every day by writing in her journal

1. Ⓨ Ⓝ

2. Circle the word that should be capitalized in the sentence.

She likes to buy journals at Barton's books and Magazines.

2. Ⓨ Ⓝ

3. Ⓨ Ⓝ

3. Underline the conjunction in sentence A below.

4. Ⓨ Ⓝ

4. Circle the contraction in sentence A below.

5. Ⓨ Ⓝ

Ⓐ She doesn't write a lot, but reading her journal helps her remember special times.

6. Ⓨ Ⓝ

5. Write the correct word for the sentence below.

___ / 6
Total

_____ find lots of journals in book stores.
(Yule, You'll, You've)

6. Circle the correctly spelled word.

faeture

feachure

feature

NAME: _____ **DATE:** _____

SCORE

1. Ⓨ Ⓝ

2. Ⓨ Ⓝ

3. Ⓨ Ⓝ

4. Ⓨ Ⓝ

5. Ⓨ Ⓝ

6. Ⓨ Ⓝ

___ / 6
Total

DIRECTIONS Read and answer each question.

1. Write the missing punctuation in the sentence.

Many people celebrate New Year's Eve on Dec 31

2. Circle the word that should be capitalized in the sentence.

Football games are popular on New Year's day.

3. Underline the prepositional phrase in sentence A below.

4. Circle the verb in sentence A below.

A Some people celebrate with gifts.

5. Write the correct word for the sentence below.

The dates _____ depending on the year.
(very, vary)

6. Circle the correctly spelled word.

recieve

receeve

receive

© Shell Education

DIRECTIONS Read and answer each question.

SCORE

1. Write the missing punctuation in the sentence.

Smokey Bear says "Only YOU can prevent forest fires!"

2. Circle the word that should be capitalized in the sentence.

The United States Forest service created Smokey.

3. Underline the adjectives in sentence A below.

4. Circle the plural noun in sentence A below.

A Wildfires can be a big problem, too.

5. Write the correct word for the sentence below.

A _____ of writers wrote a song about Smokey.
(pare, pair, pear)

6. Circle the correctly spelled word.

avoid

avode

aviod

1. Ⓨ Ⓝ

2. Ⓨ Ⓝ

3. Ⓨ Ⓝ

4. Ⓨ Ⓝ

5. Ⓨ Ⓝ

6. Ⓨ Ⓝ

___ / 6
Total

NAME: _____ DATE: _____

SCORE

1. Ⓨ Ⓝ

2. Ⓨ Ⓝ

3. Ⓨ Ⓝ

4. Ⓨ Ⓝ

5. Ⓨ Ⓝ

6. Ⓨ Ⓝ

___ / 6
Total

DIRECTIONS Read and answer each question.

1. Write the missing punctuation in the sentence.

"Lets go camping this weekend," Mom said.

2. Circle the word that should be capitalized in the sentence.

"Will you get out the tent, dad?" Mom asked.

3. Underline the conjunction in sentence A below.

4. Circle the proper noun in sentence A below.

Ⓐ Lev likes hiking and rock climbing.

5. Write the correct word for the sentence below.

Lev's dad took a picture of him standing on a huge _____.

(boulder, bolder)

6. Circle the correctly spelled word.

disaese

disease

diseace

© Shell Education

NAME: _____ DATE: _____

DIRECTIONS Read and answer each question.

1. Write the missing punctuation in the sentence.

In 1869 Wyoming gave women the right to vote.

1. Ⓨ Ⓝ

2. Circle the word that should be capitalized in the sentence.

There had been no act of congress to allow women to vote.

2. Ⓨ Ⓝ

3. Ⓨ Ⓝ

3. Underline the proper noun in sentence A below.

4. Ⓨ Ⓝ

4. Circle the plural nouns in sentence A below.

Ⓐ Women in Wyoming had to be 21 years old.

5. Ⓨ Ⓝ

6. Ⓨ Ⓝ

5. Write the correct word for the sentence below.

Wyoming was right about giving _____ the right
to vote.
(woman, women)

___ / 6
Total

6. Circle the correctly spelled word.

genuis

genius

jenius

NAME: _____ DATE: _____

SCORE

1. Ⓨ Ⓝ

2. Ⓨ Ⓝ

3. Ⓨ Ⓝ

4. Ⓨ Ⓝ

5. Ⓨ Ⓝ

6. Ⓨ Ⓝ

___ / 6
Total

DIRECTIONS Read and answer each question.

1. Write the missing punctuation in the sentence.

....
    Sarita asked, "Would you help me write a play "
....

2. Circle the word that should be capitalized in the sentence.
....
    They called the play *Bunny's basket.*
....

3. Underline the preposition in sentence A below.

4. Circle the plural noun in sentence A below.
....
  Ⓐ   The kids performed it on Teachers' Day.
....

5. Write the correct word for the sentence below.
....

  The _____ for the play was a garden.
         (scene, seen, seeing)
....

6. Circle the correctly spelled word.
....
        alreddy

        allready

        already
....

#51169—180 Days of Language
© Shell Education

NAME: _____ **DATE:** _____

DIRECTIONS Read and answer each question.

1. Write the missing punctuation in the sentence.

Chi moved to the United States from Hanoi Vietnam.

1. Ⓨ Ⓝ

2. Ⓨ Ⓝ

2. Circle the word that should be capitalized in the sentence.

Chi likes living in bridgeway.

3. Ⓨ Ⓝ

3. Underline the conjunction in sentence A below.

4. Ⓨ Ⓝ

4. Circle the verb in sentence A below.

5. Ⓨ Ⓝ

Ⓐ Chi misses his friends and relatives in Vietnam.

6. Ⓨ Ⓝ

5. Write the correct word for the sentence below.

___ / 6
Total

He _____ emails to his friends.
(rites, rights, writes)

6. Circle the correctly spelled word.

routine

ruotine

routene

NAME: _____ DATE: _____

SCORE

DIRECTIONS Read and answer each question.

1. Ⓨ Ⓝ

1. Write the missing punctuation in the sentence.

Did you ever wonder how the sandwich got its name

2. Ⓨ Ⓝ

2. Circle the word that should be capitalized in the sentence.

3. Ⓨ Ⓝ

Long ago, an earl in england stuffed some meat between two pieces of bread.

4. Ⓨ Ⓝ

3. Underline the adjectives in sentence A below.

5. Ⓨ Ⓝ

4. Circle the verb in sentence A below.

6. Ⓨ Ⓝ

Ⓐ People named the delicious idea after him, the Earl of Sandwich.

___ / 6
Total

5. Write the correct word for the sentence below.

Think about the earl _____ you eat your next sandwich.
(wile, while)

6. Circle the correctly spelled word.

delicious

delicous

deliscious

    © Shell Education

NAME: _____ **DATE:** _____

DIRECTIONS Read and answer each question.

SCORE

1. Write the missing punctuation in the sentence.

"Let's get some ice cream " Grandpa said.

1. Ⓨ Ⓝ

2. Circle the word that should be capitalized in the sentence.

"We can go to the sundae shop," gus said.

2. Ⓨ Ⓝ

3. Ⓨ Ⓝ

3. Underline the prepositional phrase in sentence A below.

4. Ⓨ Ⓝ

4. Circle the proper noun in sentence A below.

Ⓐ Gus likes vanilla ice cream on a cone.

5. Ⓨ Ⓝ

6. Ⓨ Ⓝ

5. Write the correct word for the sentence below.

"I'll have a vanilla cone, _____," Grandpa said.
(two, too, to)

___ / 6
Total

6. Circle the correctly spelled word.

prefere

prefur

prefer

NAME: _____ **DATE:** _____

SCORE

DIRECTIONS Read and answer each question.

1. (Y) (N)

1. Write the missing punctuation in the sentence.

Americas first roller coaster held 10 people in one car.

2. (Y) (N)

2. Circle the word that should be capitalized in the sentence.

3. (Y) (N)

It opened in 1884 in Coney island, New York.

4. (Y) (N)

3. Underline the prepositional phrase in sentence A below.

4. Circle the verb in sentence A below.

5. (Y) (N)

A You could ride the roller coaster for a nickel!

6. (Y) (N)

5. Write the correct word for the sentence below.

___ / 6

Total

A good roller coaster has lots of twists and _____.
(terns, turns)

6. Circle the correctly spelled word.

amuont

ammount

amount

© Shell Education

NAME: _____ **DATE:** _____

DIRECTIONS Read and answer each question.

1. Write the missing punctuation in the sentence.

Theodore Roosevelt, our 26th president loved to hunt.

2. Circle the word that should be capitalized in the sentence.

He was hunting in mississippi, and he came upon an old bear.

3. Underline the adjectives in sentence A below.

4. Circle the proper noun in sentence A below.

A Roosevelt refused to shoot the old bear.

5. Write the correct word for the sentence below.

That is why stuffed bears became _____ as teddy bears.

(now, know, known)

6. Circle the correctly spelled word.

lovuble

lovable

luvable

1. Ⓨ Ⓝ

2. Ⓨ Ⓝ

3. Ⓨ Ⓝ

4. Ⓨ Ⓝ

5. Ⓨ Ⓝ

6. Ⓨ Ⓝ

___ / 6
Total

NAME: _____ **DATE:** _____

SCORE

DIRECTIONS Read and answer each question.

1. Y N

1. Write the missing punctuation in the sentence.

Desta likes to paint with oil and Jude likes to use colored chalk.

2. Y N

2. Circle the word that should be capitalized in the sentence.

Desta likes to copy famous french artists.

3. Y N

3. Underline the conjunction in sentence A below.

4. Y N

4. Circle the contraction in sentence A below.

5. Y N

A Chalk is Jude's favorite because it's fun to draw with.

6. Y N

5. Write the correct word for the sentence below.

___ / 6
Total

Desta has _____ his paintings at an art gallery.
(show, shone, shown)

6. Circle the correctly spelled word.

ugleist

ugliest

ugilest

NAME: _____ **DATE:** _____

DIRECTIONS Read and answer each question.

1. Write the missing punctuation in the sentence.

How much would you pay for a circus elephant

1. Ⓨ Ⓝ

2. Circle the words that should be capitalized in the sentence.

P. T. barnum paid $10,000 for jumbo the elephant.

2. Ⓨ Ⓝ

3. Ⓨ Ⓝ

3. Underline the prepositional phrase in sentence A below.

4. Circle the proper noun in sentence A below.

4. Ⓨ Ⓝ

Ⓐ Jumbo was 11 feet (3 meters) tall at the shoulders.

5. Ⓨ Ⓝ

6. Ⓨ Ⓝ

5. Write the correct word for the sentence below.

Jumbo _____ 6.5 tons.
(weighed, wade, weigh)

___ / 6
Total

6. Circle the correctly spelled word.

addition

adition

additoin

NAME: _____ DATE: _____

SCORE

DIRECTIONS Read and answer each question.

1. (Y)(N)

1. Write the missing punctuation in the sentence.

"Its a great day for baseball!" Jeremy said.

2. (Y)(N)

2. Circle the word that should be capitalized in the sentence.

3. (Y)(N)

You can learn a lot about baseball in cooperstown, New York.

4. (Y)(N)

3. Underline the linking verb in sentence A below.

5. (Y)(N)

4. Circle the article in sentence A below.

A The National Baseball Hall of Fame is there.

6. (Y)(N)

5. Write the correct word for the sentence below.

___ / 6
Total

Playing on a baseball _____ can be fun!
(team, teem, meet)

6. Circle the correctly spelled word.

bonced

buonced

bounced

NAME: _____ **DATE:** _____

DIRECTIONS Read and answer each question.

1. Write the missing punctuation in the sentence.

....
In 1903 the first phone cable was laid in the Pacific Ocean.
....

1. Ⓨ Ⓝ

2. Circle the word that should be capitalized in the sentence.

....
The cable linked Honolulu and san Francisco.
....

2. Ⓨ Ⓝ

3. Ⓨ Ⓝ

3. Underline the adjectives in sentence A below.

4. Ⓨ Ⓝ

4. Circle the conjunction in sentence A below.

....
Ⓐ It was called a landline but could be called an ocean line!
....

5. Ⓨ Ⓝ

6. Ⓨ Ⓝ

5. Write the correct word for the sentence below.

....
Now, most people use _____ phones, which use satellites.
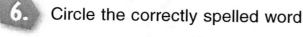
(sell, cell, sale)
....

___ / 6
Total

6. Circle the correctly spelled word.

connected

conected

conneckted

NAME: _____ **DATE:** _____

SCORE

1. Ⓨ Ⓝ

2. Ⓨ Ⓝ

3. Ⓨ Ⓝ

4. Ⓨ Ⓝ

5. Ⓨ Ⓝ

6. Ⓨ Ⓝ

___ / 6
Total

DIRECTIONS Read and answer each question.

1. Write the missing punctuation in the sentence.

Its hard to have a cold.

2. Circle the word that should be capitalized in the sentence.

Most people in the United states catch colds in the fall and winter.

3. Underline the prepositional phrase in sentence A below.

4. Circle the verb in sentence A below.

Ⓐ Kids catch six to 10 colds in a year.

5. Write the correct word for the sentence below.

_____ good news. You'll get over it in a week or two.
(There's, Theirs, Theres)

6. Circle the correctly spelled word.

powwer

power

powur

NAME: _____ DATE: _____

DIRECTIONS Read and answer each question.

1. Write the missing punctuation in the sentence.

"Guess what " cried Cerillo. "We're going to see the giraffes."

2. Circle the word that should be capitalized in the sentence.

The tallest giraffe in the world was george.

3. Underline the proper noun in sentence A below.

4. Circle the verb in sentence A below.

A He lived in a zoo in England.

5. Write the correct word for the sentence below.

Giraffes like to _____ the leaves off trees for dinner.
(peel, peal)

6. Circle the correctly spelled word.

disliek

dislike

deslike

1. Ⓨ Ⓝ

2. Ⓨ Ⓝ

3. Ⓨ Ⓝ

4. Ⓨ Ⓝ

5. Ⓨ Ⓝ

6. Ⓨ Ⓝ

___ / 6
Total

NAME: _____ **DATE:** _____

1. (Y) (N)

2. (Y) (N)

3. (Y) (N)

4. (Y) (N)

5. (Y) (N)

6. (Y) (N)

___ / 6
Total

DIRECTIONS Read and answer each question.

1. Write the missing punctuation in the sentence.

Nina, Marie, Chan, and Kim went on a scavenger hunt

2. Circle the word that should be capitalized in the sentence.

They could stop at any house on Lathrop lane.

3. Underline the linking verb in sentence A below.

4. Circle the prepositional phrase in sentence A below

A The hardest thing to find on the list was a broken skate.

5. Write the correct word for the sentence below.

They each had a _____ of pie when they were done.
(peace, piece)

6. Circle the correctly spelled word.

burdin

burdun

burden

© Shell Education

NAME: _____ **DATE:** _____

DIRECTIONS Read and answer each question.

1. Write the missing punctuation in the sentence.

....
The first U.S hot-air balloon ride was in 1793.
....

1. Ⓨ Ⓝ

2. Circle the word that should be capitalized in the sentence.

....
A man and his dog lifted up over philadelphia.
....

2. Ⓨ Ⓝ

3. Ⓨ Ⓝ

3. Underline the verb in sentence A below.

4. Ⓨ Ⓝ

4. Circle the adverb in sentence A below.

....
Ⓐ   They landed safely in Deptford, New Jersey.
....

5. Ⓨ Ⓝ

6. Ⓨ Ⓝ

5. Write the correct word for the sentence below.

....
They would not want to be hit by _____.
                                          (lightening, lightning)

____ / 6
Total

6. Circle the correctly spelled word.

....
orbit

orbut

orbitt
....

NAME: _____ **DATE:** _____

SCORE

1. Y N

2. Y N

3. Y N

4. Y N

5. Y N

6. Y N

___ / 6
Total

DIRECTIONS Read and answer each question.

1. Write the missing punctuation in the sentence.

Flying in a jet can be fun and it can also be tiring.

2. Circle the word that should be capitalized in the sentence.

Some airlines, such as ATA airlines, have closed.

3. Underline the prepositional phrase in sentence A below.

4. Underline the verbs in sentence A below.

A Pilots train for years so they fly safely.

5. Write the correct word for the sentence below.

It's also fun to fly in a small _____.
(plain, plane)

6. Circle the correctly spelled word.

motion

mochun

mocean

NAME: _____ **DATE:** _____

DIRECTIONS Read and answer each question.

1. Write the missing punctuation in the sentence.

In 1898 a quart of milk cost six cents.

1. Ⓨ Ⓝ

2. Circle the word that should be capitalized in the sentence.

Shop girls in boston made about $5.00 a week.

2. Ⓨ Ⓝ

3. Ⓨ Ⓝ

3. Underline the verb in sentence A below.

4. Ⓨ Ⓝ

4. Circle the article in sentence A below.

Ⓐ Mule drivers earned less than $3.00 a day.

5. Ⓨ Ⓝ

6. Ⓨ Ⓝ

5. Write the correct word for the sentence below.

Most people hoped someone would _____ them.
(higher, hire)

___ / 6
Total

6. Circle the correctly spelled word.

labur

labor

laibor

NAME: _____ **DATE:** _____

DIRECTIONS Read and answer each question.

1. (Y)(N)

2. (Y)(N)

3. (Y)(N)

4. (Y)(N)

5. (Y)(N)

6. (Y)(N)

___ / 6
Total

1. Write the missing punctuation in the sentence.

Have you ever been in a building with five sides

2. Circle the word that should be capitalized in the sentence.

The pentagon is a huge office building in Washington, D.C.

3. Underline the conjunction in sentence A below.

4. Circle the pronouns in sentence A below.

A It has five floors, and it has almost 8,000 windows.

5. Write the correct word for the sentence below.

Each side is 921 _____ (281 meters) long.
(feat, feet)

6. Circle the correctly spelled word.

answer

anser

ansewr

NAME: _____ **DATE:** _____

DIRECTIONS
Read and answer each question.

SCORE

1. Write the missing punctuation in the sentence.

1. Ⓨ Ⓝ

"Well go roller skating tomorrow," Pieter said.

2. Circle the word that should be capitalized in the sentence.

2. Ⓨ Ⓝ

"Let's go to the roller rink," dom said.

3. Ⓨ Ⓝ

3. Underline the verb in sentence A below.

4. Ⓨ Ⓝ

4. Circle the prepositional phrase in sentence A below.

5. Ⓨ Ⓝ

Ⓐ The kids shout loudly in the rink.

6. Ⓨ Ⓝ

5. Write the correct word for the sentence below.

___ / 6
Total

Pieter was so fast that he _____ around the rink.
(flue, flew, flu)

6. Circle the correctly spelled word.

ordur

order

ordir

NAME: _____ DATE: _____

SCORE

1. Ⓨ Ⓝ

2. Ⓨ Ⓝ

3. Ⓨ Ⓝ

4. Ⓨ Ⓝ

5. Ⓨ Ⓝ

6. Ⓨ Ⓝ

___ / 6
Total

DIRECTIONS Read and answer each question.

1. Write the missing punctuation in the sentence.

The narwhal, which is a type of whale has a very long tooth.

2. Circle the word that should be capitalized in the sentence.

Narwhals live in the coastal waters of the arctic Ocean.

3. Underline the verb in sentence A below.

4. Circle the possessive noun in sentence A below.

A The male's tooth grows more than eight feet (2 meters) long.

5. Write the correct word for the sentence below.

The tooth grows _____ the lip.
(threw, through, throw)

6. Circle the correctly spelled word.

column

colum

collumn

 © Shell Education

DIRECTIONS Read and answer each question.

SCORE

1. Write the missing punctuation in the sentence.

The female orangutan an ape, is a great mom.

1. Ⓨ Ⓝ

2. Circle the word that should be capitalized in the sentence.

Female orangutans are found in Sumatra and borneo.

2. Ⓨ Ⓝ

3. Ⓨ Ⓝ

3. Underline the verb in sentence A below.

4. Ⓨ Ⓝ

4. Circle the conjunction in sentence A below.

Ⓐ Babies stay with mom for six or seven years.

5. Ⓨ Ⓝ

6. Ⓨ Ⓝ

5. Write the correct word for the sentence below.

Mom wants to make sure they will survive on _____ own.
(there, they're, their)

_____ / 6

Total

6. Circle the correctly spelled word.

calundar

calindar

calendar

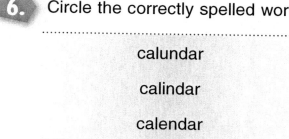

NAME: _____ DATE: _____

DIRECTIONS Read and answer each question.

1. Y N

2. Y N

3. Y N

4. Y N

5. Y N

6. Y N

___ / 6
Total

1. Write the missing punctuation in the sentence.

Elizabeth Blackwell graduated from college on January 23 1849.

2. Circle the word that should be capitalized in the sentence.

She graduated from Geneva Medical college.

3. Underline the proper noun in sentence A below.

4. Circle the linking verb in sentence A below.

A She was the first female doctor in the United States.

5. Write the correct word for the sentence below.

Take a _____, Elizabeth Blackwell!
        (bough, bow)

6. Circle the correctly spelled word.

directur

director

directer

© Shell Education

DIRECTIONS Read and answer each question.

SCORE

1. Write the missing punctuation in the sentence.

To stay healthy you need to drink plenty of water.

1. Ⓨ Ⓝ

2. Circle the word that should be capitalized in the sentence.

Planet earth has water in, on, and above it.

2. Ⓨ Ⓝ

3. Ⓨ Ⓝ

3. Underline the contraction in sentence A below.

4. Ⓨ Ⓝ

4. Circle the compound word in sentence A below.

5. Ⓨ Ⓝ

Ⓐ Water seems to be everywhere, but we can't drink it all.

6. Ⓨ Ⓝ

5. Write the correct word for the sentence below.

___ / 6
Total

Fish can live in the salty _____, but people can't.
(seas, sees, seize)

6. Circle the correctly spelled word.

glisten

glistun

glistin

NAME: _____ DATE: _____

SCORE

1. Ⓨ Ⓝ

2. Ⓨ Ⓝ

3. Ⓨ Ⓝ

4. Ⓨ Ⓝ

5. Ⓨ Ⓝ

6. Ⓨ Ⓝ

___ / 6
Total

DIRECTIONS Read and answer each question.

1. Write the missing punctuation in the sentence.

Do you think the dental drill is a new invention

2. Circle the word that should be capitalized in the sentence.

George green invented it more than 150 years ago.

3. Underline the adjective in sentence A below.

4. Circle the plural nouns in sentence A below.

Ⓐ Dentists drill out parts of teeth that are decayed.

5. Write the correct word for the sentence below.

It's better to get a cavity fixed _____ to get a tooth pulled!
(thin, then, than)

6. Circle the correctly spelled word.

difficult

diffucult

difficalt

© Shell Education

NAME: _____ **DATE:** _____

DIRECTIONS   Read and answer each question.

1. Write the missing punctuation in the sentence.

Ham, a chimpanzee flew into space in a rocket.

1. Ⓨ Ⓝ

2. Circle the word that should be capitalized in the sentence.

He was born in cameroon in 1957.

2. Ⓨ Ⓝ

3. Ⓨ Ⓝ

3. Underline the prepositional phrase in sentence A below.

4. Ⓨ Ⓝ

4. Circle the conjunction in sentence A below.

5. Ⓨ Ⓝ

Ⓐ   He wore diapers and a space suit for his flight.

6. Ⓨ Ⓝ

5. Write the correct word for the sentence below.

Ham's space suit helped keep him _____ on the flight.
(save, safe, saved)

____ / 6
Total

6. Circle the correctly spelled word.

reason

reson

reeson

NAME: _____ **DATE:** _____

SCORE

1. Y N

2. Y N

3. Y N

4. Y N

5. Y N

6. Y N

___ / 6
Total

DIRECTIONS Read and answer each question.

1. Write the missing punctuation in the sentence.

When you go to the airport do you walk on a moving sidewalk?

2. Circle the word that should be capitalized in the sentence.

The first one at an airport was at Love field in Dallas, Texas.

3. Underline the linking verb in sentence A below.

4. Circle the prepositional phrase in sentence A below.

A The length of the walkway was 1,435 feet (437 meters).

5. Write the correct word for the sentence below.

A moving sidewalk can give you a good _____.
(break, brake, breaks)

6. Circle the correctly spelled word.

elevatar

elevator

elevetor

© Shell Education

NAME: _____ **DATE:** _____

DIRECTIONS Read and answer each question.

1. Write the missing punctuation in the sentence.

Elianas favorite subject is math.

1. Ⓨ Ⓝ

2. Circle the word that should be capitalized in the sentence.

The class is taught by mr. Petersen.

2. Ⓨ Ⓝ

3. Ⓨ Ⓝ

3. Underline the adjective in sentence A below.

4. Ⓨ Ⓝ

4. Circle the verb in sentence A below.

5. Ⓨ Ⓝ

A Eliana competed in Mr. Petersen's math contest.

6. Ⓨ Ⓝ

5. Write the correct word for the sentence below.

___ / 6
Total

Eliana _____ first place and got a trophy!
(one, won, on)

6. Circle the correctly spelled word.

support

suport

suppert

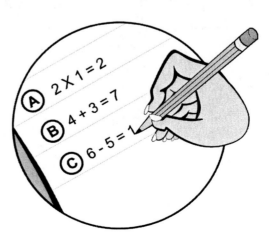

NAME: _____ **DATE:** _____

SCORE

DIRECTIONS Read and answer each question.

1. Ⓨ Ⓝ

1. Write the missing punctuation in the sentence.

....

"What is your favorite comic strip " Quinn asked.

....

2. Ⓨ Ⓝ

2. Circle the word that should be capitalized in the sentence.

....

3. Ⓨ Ⓝ

"I like *peanuts*," Declan said. "Charlie Brown is funny."

....

4. Ⓨ Ⓝ

3. Underline the verb in sentence A below.

5. Ⓨ Ⓝ

4. Circle the proper noun in sentence A below.

....

A Charles M. Schulz drew the comic strip for about 50 years.

....

6. Ⓨ Ⓝ

5. Write the correct word for the sentence below.

....

___ / 6
Total

Schulz was _____ on November 26, 1922.
              (born, bourn, borne)

....

6. Circle the correctly spelled word.

....

cartune

cartoon

cartoun

....

#51169—180 Days of Language
© Shell Education

NAME: _____ **DATE:** _____

DIRECTIONS Read and answer each question.

SCORE

1. Write the missing punctuation in the sentence.

1. Ⓨ Ⓝ

If you want to be an artist you must practice a lot.

2. Ⓨ Ⓝ

2. Circle the word that should be capitalized in the sentence.

That advice comes from tomie dePaola.

3. Ⓨ Ⓝ

3. Underline the linking verb in sentence A below.

4. Ⓨ Ⓝ

4. Circle the proper noun in sentence A below.

5. Ⓨ Ⓝ

A Mr. dePaola's name is on more than 250 books.

6. Ⓨ Ⓝ

5. Write the correct word for the sentence below.

___ / 6
Total

It also helps to take an art _____.
(course, coarse)

6. Circle the correctly spelled word.

patinet

paitent

patient

NAME: _____ **DATE:** _____

SCORE

1. Ⓨ Ⓝ

2. Ⓨ Ⓝ

3. Ⓨ Ⓝ

4. Ⓨ Ⓝ

5. Ⓨ Ⓝ

6. Ⓨ Ⓝ

___ / 6
Total

DIRECTIONS Read and answer each question.

1. Write the missing punctuation in the sentence.

If you know how to count to 26 you can write in code.

2. Circle the word that should be capitalized in the sentence.

give each letter of the alphabet a number.

3. Underline the verb in sentence A below.

4. Circle the article in sentence A below.

Ⓐ Then write a word with numbers instead of letters.

5. Write the correct word for the sentence below.

You could also use _____ instead of numbers, such as % or +.
(cymbals, symbols)

6. Circle the correctly spelled word.

invint

invent

innvent

NAME: _____ **DATE:** _____

DIRECTIONS Read and answer each question.

1. Write the missing punctuation in the sentence.

Although blinded at age three Louis Braille became famous.

2. Circle the word that should be capitalized in the sentence.

Louis braille made a system of bumps for letters.

3. Underline the prepositional phrase in sentence A below.

4. Circle the adjective in sentence A below.

A With this system, blind people could read.

5. Write the correct word for the sentence below.

Louis knew how to _____ above his troubles.
(soar, sore)

6. Circle the correctly spelled word.

succed

suceed

succeed

1. Ⓨ Ⓝ

2. Ⓨ Ⓝ

3. Ⓨ Ⓝ

4. Ⓨ Ⓝ

5. Ⓨ Ⓝ

6. Ⓨ Ⓝ

___ / 6
Total

NAME: _____ **DATE:** _____

SCORE

1. Ⓨ Ⓝ

2. Ⓨ Ⓝ

3. Ⓨ Ⓝ

4. Ⓨ Ⓝ

5. Ⓨ Ⓝ

6. Ⓨ Ⓝ

___ / 6
Total

DIRECTIONS Read and answer each question.

1. Write the missing punctuation in the sentence.

After the Civil War Louisa May Alcott wrote <u>Little Women</u>.

2. Circle the word that should be capitalized in the sentence.

During the war, she helped as a nurse in washington, D.C.

3. Underline the plural noun in sentence A below.

4. Circle the complete subject in sentence A below.

Ⓐ More than 250,000 Civil War soldiers were camped there.

5. Write the correct word for the sentence below.

There was a lot at _____ for many Americans during the war.
(steak, stake, stack)

6. Circle the correctly spelled word.

dangerous   dangerus   dangeruos

NAME: _____ DATE: _____

DIRECTIONS   Read and answer each question.

1. Write the missing punctuation in the sentence.

Pigs can be taught to fetch, sit, and spin in a circle

1. Ⓨ Ⓝ

2. Circle the word that should be capitalized in the sentence.

You may know of babe, Wilbur, or Olivia.

2. Ⓨ Ⓝ

3. Ⓨ Ⓝ

3. Underline the prepositional phrase in sentence A below.

4. Ⓨ Ⓝ

4. Circle the plural noun in sentence A below.

Ⓐ   Some pigs are trained to perform in a show.

5. Ⓨ Ⓝ

6. Ⓨ Ⓝ

5. Write the correct word for the sentence below.

It takes a lot of _____ to train a pig!
(patients, patience, patient)

___ / 6
Total

6. Circle the correctly spelled word.

discovur

discover

discovor

NAME: _____ DATE: _____

DIRECTIONS Read and answer each question.

1. (Y)(N)

1. Write the missing punctuation in the sentence.

....

Born in France Charles Perrault wrote many fairy tales.

....

2. (Y)(N)

2. Circle the word that should be capitalized in the sentence.

....

3. (Y)(N)

He wasn't the only person to write about the character cinderella.

....

4. (Y)(N)

3. Underline the adjective in sentence A below.

5. (Y)(N)

4. Circle the verbs in sentence A below.

....

6. (Y)(N)

A There are thousands of tales about different "Cinderellas" who marry princes.

....

___ / 6
Total

5. Write the correct word for the sentence below.

....

Most countries have a version of this _____.

(tale, tail)

....

6. Circle the correctly spelled word.

....

pattern

patturn

patern

....

#51169—180 Days of Language   © Shell Education

NAME: _____ **DATE:** _____

DIRECTIONS   Read and answer each question.

1. Write the missing punctuation in the sentence.

Martin Luther King Jr was born in 1928.

1. Ⓨ Ⓝ

2. Circle the word that should be capitalized in the sentence.

We celebrate his birthday on the third monday of January.

2. Ⓨ Ⓝ

3. Ⓨ Ⓝ

3. Underline the plural noun in sentence A below.

4. Ⓨ Ⓝ

4. Circle the verb in sentence A below.

Ⓐ Martin Luther King Jr. gave many fine speeches.

5. Ⓨ Ⓝ

6. Ⓨ Ⓝ

5. Write the correct word for the sentence below.

Martin Luther King Jr. was a civil _____ leader.
(rites, rights)

____ / 6
Total

6. Circle the correctly spelled word.

importunt

importent

important

NAME: _____ **DATE:** _____

SCORE

1. Ⓨ Ⓝ

2. Ⓨ Ⓝ

3. Ⓨ Ⓝ

4. Ⓨ Ⓝ

5. Ⓨ Ⓝ

6. Ⓨ Ⓝ

___ / 6
Total

DIRECTIONS Read and answer each question.

1. Write the missing punctuation in the sentence.

Cats come in all kinds of patterns such as calico, tabby, and solid.

2. Circle the word that should be capitalized in the sentence.

José likes all of his cats, but he likes mittens the most.

3. Underline the proper noun in sentence A below.

4. Circle the prepositional phrase in sentence A below.

A Boots is black except for three white paws.

5. Write the correct word for the sentence below.

Boots eats using her paws, which is _____ much fun to watch.
(so, sew, sow)

6. Circle the correctly spelled word.

dis obey

disobay

disobey

NAME: _____ **DATE:** _____

DIRECTIONS Read and answer each question.

1. Write the missing punctuation in the sentence.

In 1595 one of the first wheelchairs was made.

1. Ⓨ Ⓝ

2. Ⓨ Ⓝ

2. Circle the word that should be capitalized in the sentence.

It was made for king Phillip II of Spain.

3. Ⓨ Ⓝ

3. Underline the adjective in sentence A below.

4. Ⓨ Ⓝ

4. Circle the compound word in sentence A below.

5. Ⓨ Ⓝ

Ⓐ The wheelchair was called an invalid's chair.

6. Ⓨ Ⓝ

5. Write the correct word for the sentence below.

___ / 6
Total

Many improvements have been made since _____.
(then, than)

6. Circle the correctly spelled word.

protict

proteck

protect

NAME: _____ DATE: _____

DIRECTIONS Read and answer each question.

SCORE

1. Ⓨ Ⓝ

2. Ⓨ Ⓝ

3. Ⓨ Ⓝ

4. Ⓨ Ⓝ

5. Ⓨ Ⓝ

6. Ⓨ Ⓝ

___ / 6
Total

1. Write the missing punctuation in the sentence.

Lloyd Alexander, a famous writer said he rewrites a lot.

2. Circle the word that should be capitalized in the sentence.

One book, <u>The High King</u>, won the Newbery medal.

3. Underline the contraction in sentence A below.

4. Circle the proper noun in sentence A below.

Ⓐ Alexander said, "Some pages I've rewritten 20 times."

5. Write the correct word for the sentence below.

It _____ like a lot of work to rewrite so much.
(seems, seams)

6. Circle the correctly spelled word.

enerjy

energy

enurgy

© Shell Education

NAME: _____ DATE: _____

DIRECTIONS Read and answer each question.

1. Write the missing punctuation in the sentence.

In the 1700s, a shoemakers son ran off to sea.

2. Circle the word that should be capitalized in the sentence.

He fought with a ship's captain and was left on Mas a tierra Island.

3. Underline the proper noun in sentence A below.

4. Circle the prepositional phrase in sentence A below.

Ⓐ Alexander was rescued after nearly five years.

5. Write the correct word for the sentence below.

<u>Robinson Crusoe,</u> a book by Daniel Defoe, was _____
on Alexander's life.   (bassed, based, base)

6. Circle the correctly spelled word.

distrot

distort

destort

1. Ⓨ Ⓝ

2. Ⓨ Ⓝ

3. Ⓨ Ⓝ

4. Ⓨ Ⓝ

5. Ⓨ Ⓝ

6. Ⓨ Ⓝ

___ / 6
Total

NAME: _____ **DATE:** _____

SCORE

1. Ⓨ Ⓝ

2. Ⓨ Ⓝ

3. Ⓨ Ⓝ

4. Ⓨ Ⓝ

5. Ⓨ Ⓝ

6. Ⓨ Ⓝ

___ / 6
Total

DIRECTIONS Read and answer each question.

1. Write the missing punctuation in the sentence.

On February 2, everyones eyes are on a groundhog.

2. Circle the word that should be capitalized in the sentence.

People are encouraged to watch the sky, too, on Groundhog day.

3. Underline the conjunction in sentence A below.

4. Circle the compound word in sentence A below.

A A cloudy day means spring is close, and the groundhog stays out.

5. Write the correct word for the sentence below.

If the sky is sunny, the groundhog returns to his _____.
(whole, hole)

6. Circle the correctly spelled word.

scout

scuot

scote

  © Shell Education

NAME: _____ DATE: _____

DIRECTIONS Read and answer each question.

1. Write the missing punctuation in the sentence.

"Hurry up " Mila yelled.

1. Ⓨ Ⓝ

2. Ⓨ Ⓝ

2. Circle the word that should be capitalized in the sentence.

Mila didn't want to be late for the Veterans day parade.

3. Ⓨ Ⓝ

3. Underline the verb in sentence A below.

4. Ⓨ Ⓝ

4. Circle the preposition in sentence A below.

5. Ⓨ Ⓝ

A Mila's mom served in the army.

6. Ⓨ Ⓝ

5. Write the correct word for the sentence below.

___ / 6
Total

Mila liked to salute the flag as it _____ by.
(past, passed, pass)

6. Circle the correctly spelled word.

exellent

excelent

excellent

NAME: _____ DATE: _____

SCORE

1. Ⓨ Ⓝ

2. Ⓨ Ⓝ

3. Ⓨ Ⓝ

4. Ⓨ Ⓝ

5. Ⓨ Ⓝ

6. Ⓨ Ⓝ

___ / 6
Total

DIRECTIONS Read and answer each question.

1. Write the missing punctuation in the sentence.

Do you own two, three, or more pairs of shoes

2. Circle the word that should be capitalized in the sentence.

During world War II, there was a ration on shoes.

3. Underline the helping verb in sentence A below.

4. Circle the complete subject in sentence A below.

A People could buy three pairs of leather shoes each year.

5. Write the correct word for the sentence below.

Some people had to replace the _____ on their shoes.
                                        (souls, soles)

6. Circle the correctly spelled word.

interest

inturest

intrest

NAME: _____ **DATE:** _____

DIRECTIONS Read and answer each question.

1. Write the missing punctuation in the sentence.

1. Ⓨ Ⓝ

In 1908 a penny could buy a lot.

2. Ⓨ Ⓝ

2. Circle the word that should be capitalized in the sentence.

You could mail a letter anywhere in the United states for a penny.

3. Ⓨ Ⓝ

3. Underline the plural noun in sentence A below.

4. Ⓨ Ⓝ

4. Circle the verbs in sentence A below.

5. Ⓨ Ⓝ

A Ask your parents what a postage stamp cost the year of your birth.

6. Ⓨ Ⓝ

5. Write the correct word for the sentence below.

___ / 6
Total

Stamps today cost a lot more than one _____!
(scent, sent, cent)

6. Circle the correctly spelled word.

broaght

brought

brout

NAME: _____ DATE: _____

SCORE

DIRECTIONS Read and answer each question.

1. Ⓨ Ⓝ

1. Write the missing punctuation in the sentence.

"Do you pay attention to what you eat " Ms Tomez asked.

2. Ⓨ Ⓝ

2. Circle the word that should be capitalized in the sentence.

3. Ⓨ Ⓝ

"Most of us don't," ms. Tomez said.

4. Ⓨ Ⓝ

3. Underline the contraction in sentence A below.

5. Ⓨ Ⓝ

4. Circle the conjunction in sentence A below.

6. Ⓨ Ⓝ

 "Keep a diary, and you'll learn a lot," she told the class.

____ / 6
Total

5. Write the correct word for the sentence below.

Your health will be better if you _____ good food.
                                    (chews, choose, choice)

6. Circle the correctly spelled word.

plentiful

plentifull

plentifil

© Shell Education

NAME: _____ **DATE:** _____

| DIRECTIONS | Read and answer each question. |

1. Write the missing punctuation in the sentence.

When you go to the zoo what animals do you visit?

1. Ⓨ Ⓝ

2. Circle the word that should be capitalized in the sentence.

The african lion is called a "vulnerable" lion.

2. Ⓨ Ⓝ

3. Ⓨ Ⓝ

3. Underline the prepositional phrase in sentence A below.

4. Ⓨ Ⓝ

4. Circle the plural noun in sentence A below.

5. Ⓨ Ⓝ

A *Vulnerable* means that the lions are in danger.

6. Ⓨ Ⓝ

5. Write the correct word for the sentence below.

___ / 6
Total

_____ much of the land is being used by people.
(To, Two, Too)

6. Circle the correctly spelled word.

tracktor

tracter

tractor

NAME: _____ **DATE:** _____

1. Ⓨ Ⓝ

2. Ⓨ Ⓝ

3. Ⓨ Ⓝ

4. Ⓨ Ⓝ

5. Ⓨ Ⓝ

6. Ⓨ Ⓝ

___ / 6
Total

DIRECTIONS Read and answer each question.

1. Write the missing punctuation in the sentence.

....

We could go to a movie but I prefer bowling.

....

2. Circle the word that should be capitalized in the sentence.

....

We could use a coupon for a free game at Joe's lanes.

....

3. Underline the possessive pronoun in sentence A below.

4. Circle the verb in sentence A below.

....

Ⓐ His snack bar has great hot dogs.

....

5. Write the correct word for the sentence below.

....

No one likes to _____ a gutter ball!
             (role, roll, rolled)

....

6. Circle the correctly spelled word.

....

nuisanse

nuisence

nuisance

© Shell Education

NAME: _____ **DATE:** _____

DIRECTIONS Read and answer each question.

1. Write the missing punctuation in the sentence.

Wait I want to try to win a prize!

1. Ⓨ Ⓝ

2. Circle the word that should be capitalized in the sentence.

The man at the booth handed dad a baseball.

2. Ⓨ Ⓝ

3. Ⓨ Ⓝ

3. Underline the prepositional phrase in sentence A below.

4. Ⓨ Ⓝ

4. Circle the verb in sentence A below.

Ⓐ Dad pitched the ball at the bottles.

5. Ⓨ Ⓝ

6. Ⓨ Ⓝ

5. Write the correct word for the sentence below.

"You _____!" Joey shouted.
(one, wind, won)

___ / 6
Total

6. Circle the correctly spelled word.

equel

equal

eqaul

NAME: _____ **DATE:** _____

SCORE

1. (Y)(N)

2. (Y)(N)

3. (Y)(N)

4. (Y)(N)

5. (Y)(N)

6. (Y)(N)

___ / 6
Total

DIRECTIONS Read and answer each question.

1. Write the missing punctuation in the sentence.

Do you know what you can find in Wyoming, Montana, and Idaho

2. Circle the word that should be capitalized in the sentence.

You can visit Yellowstone National park there.

3. Underline the plural noun in sentence A below.

4. Circle the contraction in sentence A below.

A Don't feed the animals if you go there.

5. Write the correct word for the sentence below.

You don't want to get a _____ mad!
                                    (bear, bare)

6. Circle the correctly spelled word.

mound

mond

mownd

© Shell Education

NAME: _____ **DATE:** _____

DIRECTIONS Read and answer each question.

1. Write the missing punctuation in the sentence.

In 1853 three brothers quit their jobs.

1. Ⓨ Ⓝ

2. Circle the word that should be capitalized in the sentence.

They started a piano company called Steinway & sons.

2. Ⓨ Ⓝ

3. Ⓨ Ⓝ

3. Underline the plural noun in sentence A below.

4. Ⓨ Ⓝ

4. Circle the article in sentence A below.

Ⓐ Now, the company makes more than 2,000 pianos each year.

5. Ⓨ Ⓝ

6. Ⓨ Ⓝ

5. Write the correct word for the sentence below.

_____ company makes some of the finest pianos in the world.
(They're, There, Their)

___ / 6
Total

6. Circle the correctly spelled word.

peddal

pedle

pedal

NAME: _____ **DATE:** _____

SCORE

DIRECTIONS Read and answer each question.

1. (Y)(N)

1. Write the missing punctuation in the sentence.

Washington Irving, born in 1783 was a writer.

2. (Y)(N)

2. Circle the word that should be capitalized in the sentence.

3. (Y)(N)

Irving wrote about a man called Rip van Winkle.

4. (Y)(N)

3. Underline the preposition in sentence A below.

5. (Y)(N)

4. Circle the proper noun in sentence A below.

A Rip slept for 20 years!

6. (Y)(N)

5. Write the correct word for the sentence below.

___ / 6
Total

What would you _____ first after that long nap?
(due, do, dew)

6. Circle the correctly spelled word.

breathe

breeth

bearth

© Shell Education

NAME: _____ **DATE:** _____

> **DIRECTIONS** Read and answer each question.

SCORE

1. Write the missing punctuation in the sentence.

"Let's plant a tree for Arbor Day " Malia said.

1. Ⓨ Ⓝ

2. Ⓨ Ⓝ

2. Circle the word that should be capitalized in the sentence.

The first Arbor Day, in 1872, was in nebraska.

3. Ⓨ Ⓝ

3. Underline the verb in sentence A below.

4. Ⓨ Ⓝ

4. Circle the proper noun in sentence A below.

Ⓐ People around the world plant trees on Arbor Day.

5. Ⓨ Ⓝ

6. Ⓨ Ⓝ

5. Write the correct word for the sentence below.

___/ 6
Total

_____ fun to watch a tree grow.
(Its, It's)

6. Circle the correctly spelled word.

nature

nachere

natere

NAME: _____ **DATE:** _____

DIRECTIONS Read and answer each question.

SCORE

1. Ⓨ Ⓝ

2. Ⓨ Ⓝ

3. Ⓨ Ⓝ

4. Ⓨ Ⓝ

5. Ⓨ Ⓝ

6. Ⓨ Ⓝ

___ / 6
Total

1. Write the missing punctuation in the sentence.

If you live in New York City you may call this game *Potsy*.

2. Circle the word that should be capitalized in the sentence.

Hopscotch is called *escargot* in france, which means "snail."

3. Underline the conjunction in sentence A below.

4. Circle the contraction in sentence A below.

A Don't step on a line or lose your balance!

5. Write the correct word for the sentence below.

If you have a _____ of chalk and a rock, you can play the game.   (piece, peace)

6. Circle the correctly spelled word.

ojbect

object

objict

NAME: _____ **DATE:** _____

| DIRECTIONS | Read and answer each question. |

1. Write the missing punctuation in the sentence.

Do you ever look in the attic for old or hidden things

1. Ⓨ Ⓝ

2. Circle the word that should be capitalized in the sentence.

You might want to visit Mr. Topper's Treasure chest.

2. Ⓨ Ⓝ

3. Ⓨ Ⓝ

3. Underline the conjunction in sentence A below.

4. Ⓨ Ⓝ

4. Circle the contraction in sentence A below.

5. Ⓨ Ⓝ

A You'll find toys, jewelry, comic books, and more.

6. Ⓨ Ⓝ

5. Write the correct word for the sentence below.

___ / 6
Total

It's best to shop when there's a _____.
(sail, sale, sell)

6. Circle the correctly spelled word.

celler

cellur

cellar

NAME: _____ DATE: _____

DIRECTIONS Read and answer each question.

1. Ⓨ Ⓝ

1. Write the missing punctuation in the sentence.

In 1997 a boa constrictor died at over 40 years old.

2. Ⓨ Ⓝ

2. Circle the word that should be capitalized in the sentence.

3. Ⓨ Ⓝ

The boa, named Popeye, lived at the Philadelphia zoo.

4. Ⓨ Ⓝ

3. Underline the verb in sentence A below.

4. Circle the nouns in sentence A below.

5. Ⓨ Ⓝ

A Most boa constrictors live 20 to 30 years.

6. Ⓨ Ⓝ

5. Write the correct word for the sentence below.

___ / 6
Total

Boa constrictors squeeze their _____ to death.
(prey, pray)

6. Circle the correctly spelled word.

motife

motive

mottive

NAME: _____ **DATE:** _____

DIRECTIONS Read and answer each question.

1. Write the missing punctuation in the sentence.

"Chocolate is my favorite treat," said Tanesha

2. Circle the word that should be capitalized in the sentence.

"I visited hershey, Pennsylvania, once," said Ben.

3. Underline the prepositional phrase in sentence A below.

4. Circle the pronoun in sentence A below.

A "You could smell chocolate from the factory," Ben added.

5. Write the correct word for the sentence below.

"I'd ask for chocolate for _____," Tanesha said.
                                                    (dessert, desert)

6. Circle the correctly spelled word.

scend

secnt

scent

1. Ⓨ Ⓝ

2. Ⓨ Ⓝ

3. Ⓨ Ⓝ

4. Ⓨ Ⓝ

5. Ⓨ Ⓝ

6. Ⓨ Ⓝ

___ / 6
Total

NAME: _____ DATE: _____

SCORE

DIRECTIONS Read and answer each question.

1. Ⓨ Ⓝ

1. Write the missing punctuation in the sentence.
....
Do you use ice skates, in-line skates, or roller skates
....

2. Ⓨ Ⓝ

2. Circle the word that should be capitalized in the sentence.
....
Skates were used in holland hundreds of years ago.
....

3. Ⓨ Ⓝ

4. Ⓨ Ⓝ

3. Underline the proper noun in sentence A below.

5. Ⓨ Ⓝ

4. Circle the verbs in sentence A below.
....

6. Ⓨ Ⓝ

Ⓐ Dutchmen attached spools to their shoes so they could skate on land.
....

___ / 6
Total

5. Write the correct word for the sentence below.
....
Today's ice skate blades are made of _____.
(steel, steal)
....

6. Circle the correctly spelled word.
....
scisors

scissors

scissers
....

© Shell Education

NAME: _____ **DATE:** _____

DIRECTIONS Read and answer each question.

SCORE

1. Write the missing punctuation in the sentence.

1. (Y)(N)

An Easter Egg Roll was held by President Rutherford B Hayes.

2. (Y)(N)

2. Circle the word that should be capitalized in the sentence.

It was held at the white House in 1878.

3. (Y)(N)

3. Underline the article in sentence A below.

4. (Y)(N)

4. Circle the proper noun in sentence A below.

5. (Y)(N)

A It is still held the day after Easter.

6. (Y)(N)

5. Write the correct word for the sentence below.

___/6
Total

_____ you like to go to the Easter Egg Roll?
(Would, Wood)

6. Circle the correctly spelled word.

collection

colection

collectoin

NAME: _____ **DATE:** _____

SCORE

1. Ⓨ Ⓝ

2. Ⓨ Ⓝ

3. Ⓨ Ⓝ

4. Ⓨ Ⓝ

5. Ⓨ Ⓝ

6. Ⓨ Ⓝ

___ / 6
Total

DIRECTIONS   Read and answer each question.

1. Write the missing punctuation in the sentence.

For decades many people have worried about whales.

2. Circle the word that should be capitalized in the sentence.

World Whale day began in 1975.

3. Underline the prepositional phrase in sentence A below.

4. Circle the plural noun in sentence A below.

A   These large mammals are being killed for food.

5. Write the correct word for the sentence below.

It would be sad to see these animals _____ out.
(die, dye)

6. Circle the correctly spelled word.

ocean

occean

ocaen

NAME: _____ **DATE:** _____

DIRECTIONS Read and answer each question.

1. Write the missing punctuation in the sentence.

On May 5 1961, the first American entered outer space.

2. Circle the word that should be capitalized in the sentence.

Alan shepard shot into space as part of the Mercury Project.

3. Underline the plural noun in sentence A below.

4. Circle the preposition in sentence A below.

A The *Freedom 7* reached an altitude of 116 miles (187 kilometers).

5. Write the correct word for the sentence below.

Many astronauts _____ in space after that first flight.

(flue, flew, flu)

6. Circle the correctly spelled word.

horizen

horizzen

horizon

1. Ⓨ Ⓝ

2. Ⓨ Ⓝ

3. Ⓨ Ⓝ

4. Ⓨ Ⓝ

5. Ⓨ Ⓝ

6. Ⓨ Ⓝ

___ / 6
Total

NAME: _____ **DATE:** _____

DIRECTIONS Read and answer each question.

SCORE

1. Ⓨ Ⓝ

2. Ⓨ Ⓝ

3. Ⓨ Ⓝ

4. Ⓨ Ⓝ

5. Ⓨ Ⓝ

6. Ⓨ Ⓝ

___ / 6
Total

1. Write the missing punctuation in the sentence.

A coffin may be made of wood but some are made of gold.

2. Circle the word that should be capitalized in the sentence.

In ancient egypt, a king's coffin might be covered with gold.

3. Underline the proper noun in sentence A below.

4. Circle the verb in sentence A below.

A One tomb, for King Tut, had a solid gold coffin.

5. Write the correct word for the sentence below.

King Tut _____ bandages inside of the coffin.
(wore, war, wear)

6. Circle the correctly spelled word.

death

deeth

deuth

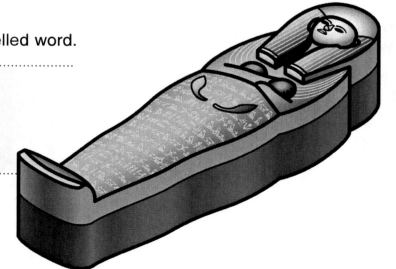

NAME: _____ **DATE:** _____

DIRECTIONS Read and answer each question.

1. Write the missing punctuation in the sentence

Railroads built on dirt roads have been around for a long time

1. Ⓨ Ⓝ

2. Circle the word that should be capitalized in the sentence.

In the 1700s, europeans began to use iron rails.

2. Ⓨ Ⓝ

3. Ⓨ Ⓝ

3. Underline the helping verb in sentence A below.

4. Ⓨ Ⓝ

4. Circle the article in sentence A below.

Ⓐ However, the carts were pulled by horses!

5. Ⓨ Ⓝ

6. Ⓨ Ⓝ

5. Write the correct word for the sentence below.

Steams engines were not _____ until the 1700s.

(maid, made, mad)

___ / 6
Total

6. Circle the correctly spelled word.

distriked

district

districk

NAME: _____ DATE: _____

SCORE

1. Ⓨ Ⓝ

2. Ⓨ Ⓝ

3. Ⓨ Ⓝ

4. Ⓨ Ⓝ

5. Ⓨ Ⓝ

6. Ⓨ Ⓝ

___ / 6
Total

DIRECTIONS Read and answer each question.

1. Write the missing punctuation in the sentence.

How far could you drive on three gallons of gas

2. Circle the word that should be capitalized in the sentence.

that's how much gas people got for a week during World War II.

3. Underline the preposition in sentence A below.

4. Circle the compound subject in sentence A below.

Ⓐ Sugar and coffee were rationed during the war, too.

5. Write the correct word for the sentence below.

People had to learn to get _____ with less.
(by, buy, bye)

6. Circle the correctly spelled word.

affurd

aford

afford

© Shell Education

NAME: _____ DATE: _____

DIRECTIONS Read and answer each question.

1. Write the missing punctuation in the sentence.

1. Ⓨ Ⓝ

You don't have to be Irish to celebrate St Patrick's Day.

2. Ⓨ Ⓝ

2. Circle the word that should be capitalized in the sentence.

In Chicago, the Chicago river is dyed green.

3. Ⓨ Ⓝ

3. Underline the introductory phrase in sentence A below.

4. Ⓨ Ⓝ

4. Circle the articles in sentence A below.

5. Ⓨ Ⓝ

Ⓐ In 1962, the water was green for a week!

6. Ⓨ Ⓝ

5. Write the correct word for the sentence below.

___ / 6
Total

Now they use less vegetable _____, and it's green for a few hours.
(die, dye, dyed)

6. Circle the correctly spelled word.

weeve

weave

waeve

NAME: _____ **DATE:** _____

SCORE

1. Ⓨ Ⓝ

2. Ⓨ Ⓝ

3. Ⓨ Ⓝ

4. Ⓨ Ⓝ

5. Ⓨ Ⓝ

6. Ⓨ Ⓝ

___ / 6
Total

DIRECTIONS Read and answer each question.

1. Write the missing punctuation in the sentence.

Sol likes to grow pumpkins and he likes carrots, too.

2. Circle the word that should be capitalized in the sentence.

He entered his pumpkin in a contest at the County fair.

3. Underline the proper noun in sentence A below.

4. Circle the pronouns in sentence A below.

A He was excited when his pumpkin was named "Biggest County Pumpkin."

5. Write the correct word for the sentence below.

The judge said, "That pumpkin _____ 30 pounds (14 kilograms)!"   (weighs, ways, weigh)

6. Circle the correctly spelled word.

except

exsept

eccept

NAME: _____ **DATE:** _____

DIRECTIONS Read and answer each question.

1. Write the missing punctuation in the sentence.

Some frogs jump really high and some frogs jump really far.

2. Circle the word that should be capitalized in the sentence.

One frog in south Africa was in a frog derby.

3. Underline the proper noun in sentence A below.

4. Circle the conjunction in sentence A below.

Ⓐ Santjie was in the triple jump and jumped more than 33 feet (10 meters)!

5. Write the correct word for the sentence below.

_____ quite a talented frog!
    (Its, It's)

6. Circle the correctly spelled word.

buseist

busiest

bisiest

1. Ⓨ Ⓝ

2. Ⓨ Ⓝ

3. Ⓨ Ⓝ

4. Ⓨ Ⓝ

5. Ⓨ Ⓝ

6. Ⓨ Ⓝ

___ / 6
Total

NAME: _____ DATE: _____

SCORE

1. Ⓨ Ⓝ

2. Ⓨ Ⓝ

3. Ⓨ Ⓝ

4. Ⓨ Ⓝ

5. Ⓨ Ⓝ

6. Ⓨ Ⓝ

___ / 6
Total

DIRECTIONS Read and answer each question.

1. Write the missing punctuation in the sentence.

Zoe, who is going to the theater asked her friends to come, too.

2. Circle the word that should be capitalized in the sentence.

They want to see Clara perform in *annie*.

3. Underline the prepositional phrase in sentence A below.

4. Circle the contraction in sentence A below.

Ⓐ They don't want to be late for the opening curtain.

5. Write the correct word for the sentence below.

They _____ the bus and got there right on time.
(rowed, rode, road)

6. Circle the correctly spelled word.

remember

remembur

reemember

    © Shell Education

NAME: _____ **DATE:** _____

> **DIRECTIONS** Read and answer each question.

1. Write the missing punctuation in the sentence.

Jane Yolen was born on February 11 1939.

1. Ⓨ Ⓝ

2. Circle the word that should be capitalized in the sentence.

Many young readers love her Commander toad series.

2. Ⓨ Ⓝ

3. Ⓨ Ⓝ

3. Underline the prepositional phrase in sentence A below.

4. Ⓨ Ⓝ

4. Circle the proper noun in sentence A below.

Ⓐ Yolen sold her first book at age 22.

5. Ⓨ Ⓝ

6. Ⓨ Ⓝ

5. Write the correct word for the sentence below.

Yolen _____ all kinds of books, from novels to poetry.
(rites, rights, writes)

___ / 6
Total

6. Circle the correctly spelled word.

expurt

egspert

expert

© Shell Education

NAME: _____ DATE: _____

SCORE

1. Ⓨ Ⓝ

2. Ⓨ Ⓝ

3. Ⓨ Ⓝ

4. Ⓨ Ⓝ

5. Ⓨ Ⓝ

6. Ⓨ Ⓝ

___ / 6
Total

DIRECTIONS Read and answer each question.

1. Write the missing punctuation in the sentence.

....

If you could fly anywhere on your birthday where would you go?

....

2. Circle the word that should be capitalized in the sentence.

....

Would you fly to Paris, rome, or London?

....

3. Underline the contraction in sentence A below.

4. Circle the pronoun in sentence A below.

....

A If you can't travel, read a book about a faraway place.

....

5. Write the correct word for the sentence below.

....

It's fun to _____ new people when traveling.
          (meet, meat, mete)

....

6. Circle the correctly spelled word.

....

distent

distant

ditstant

#51169—180 Days of Language   © Shell Education

NAME: _____ **DATE:** _____

DIRECTIONS Read and answer each question.

1. Write the missing punctuation in the sentence.

If you have tennis shoes you probably have aglets.

2. Circle the word that should be capitalized in the sentence.

The modern shoestring was invented in england in 1790.

3. Underline the prepositions in sentence A below.

4. Circle the complete subject in sentence A below.

A   An aglet is the plastic tube at the end of each lace.

5. Write the correct word for the sentence below.

The aglet helps you thread the shoelace _____
the opening.
(through, threw, thou)

6. Circle the correctly spelled word.

bukkle

buckel

buckle

1. Ⓨ Ⓝ

2. Ⓨ Ⓝ

3. Ⓨ Ⓝ

4. Ⓨ Ⓝ

5. Ⓨ Ⓝ

6. Ⓨ Ⓝ

___ / 6
Total

NAME: _____ DATE: _____

DIRECTIONS Read and answer each question.

1. Y N

1. Write the missing punctuation in the sentence.

....

"Write what you know " writers often say.

....

2. Y N

2. Circle the word that should be capitalized in the sentence.

....

however, you must use your imagination to write about aliens.

....

3. Y N

3. Underline the adjectives in sentence A below.

4. Y N

4. Circle the plural nouns in sentence A below.

....

5. Y N

A My favorite books are about aliens.

....

6. Y N

5. Write the correct word for the sentence below.

....

___ / 6
Total

I read _____ books about aliens last month!
                (for, fore, four)

....

6. Circle the correctly spelled word.

....

portion

porton

porchun

....

© Shell Education

DIRECTIONS Read and answer each question.

SCORE

1. Write the missing punctuation in the sentence.

"My dog ate my homework used to be a common excuse.

1. Ⓨ Ⓝ

2. Circle the word that should be capitalized in the sentence.

Now, kids can say, "my computer crashed."

2. Ⓨ Ⓝ

3. Ⓨ Ⓝ

3. Underline the adjectives in sentence A below.

4. Ⓨ Ⓝ

4. Circle the contraction in sentence A below.

Ⓐ It's wise to have at least one backup plan.

5. Ⓨ Ⓝ

6. Ⓨ Ⓝ

5. Write the correct word for the sentence below.

Be sure you have enough computer memory, or _____, too.
(bites, bytes, bights)

___ / 6
Total

6. Circle the correctly spelled word.

folish

foolish

foulish

NAME: _____ DATE: _____

DIRECTIONS Read and answer each question.

1. Y N

1. Write the missing punctuation in the sentence.

Mark Twain, who wrote <u>The Adventures of Tom Sawyer</u> loved cats.

2. Y N

2. Circle the word that should be capitalized in the sentence.

He named one of them Stray kit.

3. Y N

3. Underline the verb in sentence A below.

4. Y N

4. Circle the possessive noun in sentence A below.

Ⓐ Twain's mother owned 20 cats!

5. Y N

5. Write the correct word for the sentence below.

6. Y N

You'd never be _____ with 20 cats in your house!

(bored, board)

___ / 6
Total

6. Circle the correctly spelled word.

porchhe

pourch

porch

© Shell Education

NAME: _____ **DATE:** _____

DIRECTIONS Read and answer each question.

1. Write the missing punctuation in the sentence.

1. Ⓨ Ⓝ

Have you heard of Pecos Bill, Widow-Maker and Slue-Foot Sue?

2. Ⓨ Ⓝ

2. Circle the word that should be capitalized in the sentence.

3. Ⓨ Ⓝ

Pecos Bill first saw Sue riding a catfish down the Rio grande.

4. Ⓨ Ⓝ

3. Underline the conjunction in sentence A below

4. Circle the possessive noun in sentence A below.

5. Ⓨ Ⓝ

Ⓐ Widow-maker was Bill's horse, and Sue wanted to ride it.

6. Ⓨ Ⓝ

5. Write the correct word for the sentence below.

___ / 6
Total

Sue rode it but was _____ off and bounced up to the moon.
(thrown, throne)

6. Circle the correctly spelled word.

probubly

prabably

probably

NAME: _____ DATE: _____

DIRECTIONS Read and answer each question.

SCORE

1. (Y)(N)

2. (Y)(N)

3. (Y)(N)

4. (Y)(N)

5. (Y)(N)

6. (Y)(N)

___ / 6
Total

1. Write the missing punctuation in the sentence.

"It's time to sign up for the spelling bee," Mr Lucero announced.

2. Circle the word that should be capitalized in the sentence.

"It's sponsored by the newspaper *City news*," he added.

3. Underline the verbs in sentence A below.

4. Circle the prepositional phrase in sentence A below.

A Spellers spell and define words at this year's contest.

5. Write the correct word for the sentence below.

If you have a _____ for spelling, try competing some time.
(flare, flair)

6. Circle the correctly spelled word.

mispelled

misspelled

mispeled

NAME: _____ **DATE:** _____

DIRECTIONS Read and answer each question.

1. Write the missing punctuation in the sentence.

"Look There's a covey of quail outside!" Alma cried.

1. Ⓨ Ⓝ

2. Ⓨ Ⓝ

2. Circle the word that should be capitalized in the sentence.

Quail sometimes sound like they are saying, "chicago."

3. Ⓨ Ⓝ

3. Underline the plural nouns in sentence A below.

4. Ⓨ Ⓝ

4. Circle the adjective in sentence A below.

5. Ⓨ Ⓝ

Ⓐ Quail like to take dust baths.

6. Ⓨ Ⓝ

5. Write the correct word for the sentence below.

___ / 6
Total

They _____ in the dirt and flap their wings.
(burro, burrow, borough)

6. Circle the correctly spelled word.

haich

hatch

hacth

NAME: _____ DATE: _____

SCORE

1. Ⓨ Ⓝ

2. Ⓨ Ⓝ

3. Ⓨ Ⓝ

4. Ⓨ Ⓝ

5. Ⓨ Ⓝ

6. Ⓨ Ⓝ

___ / 6
Total

DIRECTIONS Read and answer each question.

1. Write the missing punctuation in the sentence.

During the mid-1800s Harriet Tubman helped many slaves escape.

2. Circle the word that should be capitalized in the sentence.

The Underground railroad was not a real railroad.

3. Underline the plural noun in sentence A below.

4. Circle the conjunction in sentence A below.

Ⓐ People bravely hid the slaves and took them north to freedom.

5. Write the correct word for the sentence below.

Her burial _____ is in Auburn, New York.
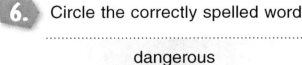
(sight, site, sighed)

6. Circle the correctly spelled word.

dangerous

dangerus

dangeruos

© Shell Education

NAME: _____ **DATE:** _____

> **DIRECTIONS** Read and answer each question.

1. Write the missing punctuation in the sentence.

You may not know the name Andrew Lang but you have probably read his work.

1. Ⓨ Ⓝ

2. Ⓨ Ⓝ

2. Circle the word that should be capitalized in the sentence.

He collected fairy tales, starting with <u>The Blue Fairy book</u>.

3. Ⓨ Ⓝ

3. Underline the prepositional phrase in sentence A below.

4. Ⓨ Ⓝ

4. Circle the pronoun in sentence A below.

5. Ⓨ Ⓝ

Ⓐ He used different colors for all the titles.

6. Ⓨ Ⓝ

5. Write the correct word for the sentence below.

___ / 6
Total

He said that children _____ what is true and what is
make-believe. (know, no, now)

6. Circle the correctly spelled word.

argud

argeud

argued

NAME: _____ **DATE:** _____

SCORE

1. Ⓨ Ⓝ

2. Ⓨ Ⓝ

3. Ⓨ Ⓝ

4. Ⓨ Ⓝ

5. Ⓨ Ⓝ

6. Ⓨ Ⓝ

___ / 6
Total

DIRECTIONS Read and answer each question.

1. Write the missing punctuation in the sentence.

....

Do you like reading book series such as Harry Potter

....

2. Circle the word that should be capitalized in the sentence.

....

The Chronicles of narnia is also a great book series.

....

3. Underline the verb in sentence A below.

4. Circle the plural nouns in sentence A below.

....

Ⓐ Readers wait excitedly for new books in a series.

....

5. Write the correct word for the sentence below.

....

_____ nothing better than starting a great new book!

(Theirs, There's, There're)

....

6. Circle the correctly spelled word.

....

favorite

favorete

favurite

....

© Shell Education

NAME: _____ **DATE:** _____

DIRECTIONS Read and answer each question.

1. Write the missing punctuation in the sentence.

> During the Great Depression a man invented a new board game.

1. Ⓨ Ⓝ

2. Ⓨ Ⓝ

2. Circle the word that should be capitalized in the sentence.

> He sold the game to macy's department store.

3. Ⓨ Ⓝ

3. Underline the verb in sentence A below.

4. Ⓨ Ⓝ

4. Circle the pronoun in sentence A below.

5. Ⓨ Ⓝ

> **A** You have probably played this word game.

6. Ⓨ Ⓝ

5. Write the correct word for the sentence below.

___/ 6

Total

> Playing Scrabble™ is a _____ way to have fun and learn new words.
>   (great, grate)

6. Circle the correctly spelled word.

> brane
>
> brain
>
> braen

NAME: _____ DATE: _____

DIRECTIONS Read and answer each question.

1. Ⓨ Ⓝ

1. Write the missing punctuation in the sentence.

In 1828 the first American dictionary was published.

2. Ⓨ Ⓝ

2. Circle the word that should be capitalized in the sentence.

3. Ⓨ Ⓝ

Noah webster spent 22 years writing it.

4. Ⓨ Ⓝ

3. Underline the plural noun in sentence A below.

5. Ⓨ Ⓝ

4. Circle the possessive pronoun in sentence A below.

Ⓐ What would he think of seeing his dictionary on computers?

6. Ⓨ Ⓝ

5. Write the correct word for the sentence below.

___ / 6
Total

_____ you spend 22 years writing one book?
(Would, Wood)

6. Circle the correctly spelled word.

rought

roagh

rough

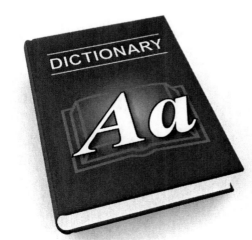

 #51169—180 Days of Language © Shell Education

NAME: _____ **DATE:** _____

DIRECTIONS Read and answer each question.

SCORE

1. Write the missing punctuation in the sentence.

If you want to run in the biggest race go to the Big Apple.

1. Ⓨ Ⓝ

2. Circle the word that should be capitalized in the sentence.

More than 40,000 people race in the New York city Marathon.

2. Ⓨ Ⓝ

3. Ⓨ Ⓝ

3. Underline the prepositional phrase in sentence A below.

4. Ⓨ Ⓝ

4. Circle the contraction in sentence A below.

5. Ⓨ Ⓝ

A You'll be running for 26.2 miles (42 kilometers).

6. Ⓨ Ⓝ

5. Write the correct word for the sentence below.

___ / 6
Total

Crossing the finish line is quite a _____.

(feet, feat)

6. Circle the correctly spelled word.

positon

position

positoin

NAME: _____ DATE: _____

SCORE

1. Ⓨ Ⓝ

2. Ⓨ Ⓝ

3. Ⓨ Ⓝ

4. Ⓨ Ⓝ

5. Ⓨ Ⓝ

6. Ⓨ Ⓝ

___ / 6
Total

DIRECTIONS Read and answer each question.

1. Write the missing punctuation in the sentence.

....

When you want water do you turn on a faucet?

....

2. Circle the word that should be capitalized in the sentence.

....

In parts of africa, women and children haul water in jugs.

....

3. Underline the prepositional phrases in sentence A below.

4. Circle the possessive pronoun in sentence A below.

....

A They may walk for hours with their heavy jugs.

....

5. Write the correct word for the sentence below.

....

Water is very scarce in the _____.
                                    (desert, dessert)

....

6. Circle the correctly spelled word.

....

trouble

truoble

troubel

....

  © Shell Education

NAME: _____ **DATE:** _____

SCORE

| DIRECTIONS | Read and answer each question. |

1. Write the missing punctuation in the sentence.

If you like dog stories be sure to read <u>Old Yeller</u>.

1. Ⓨ Ⓝ

2. Circle the words that should be capitalized in the sentence.

It was written by fred gipson and was a Newbery Honor book.

2. Ⓨ Ⓝ

3. Ⓨ Ⓝ

3. Underline the prepositional phrase in sentence A below.

4. Ⓨ Ⓝ

4. Circle the conjunction in sentence A below.

Ⓐ Next, watch the movie and compare it to the book.

5. Ⓨ Ⓝ

6. Ⓨ Ⓝ

5. Write the correct word for the sentence below.

What _____ does Travis learn from Old Yeller?
(lessen, lesson)

___ / 6
Total

6. Circle the correctly spelled word.

several

severel

severral

NAME: _____ DATE: _____

SCORE

DIRECTIONS Read and answer each question.

1. (Y) (N)

1. Write the missing punctuation in the sentence.

The first car built by Henry Ford was finished on June 4 1896.

2. (Y) (N)

2. Circle the word that should be capitalized in the sentence.

3. (Y) (N)

It was built in a shed in detroit, and there was a problem.

4. (Y) (N)

3. Underline the plural noun in sentence A below.

5. (Y) (N)

4. Circle the preposition in sentence A below.

A The car was wider than the doors on the shed!

6. (Y) (N)

5. Write the correct word for the sentence below.

___ / 6
Total

How do you think they solved _____ problem?
(they're, there, their)

6. Circle the correctly spelled word.

difficultey

difficulty

diffaculty

© Shell Education

NAME: _____ **DATE:** _____

DIRECTIONS Read and answer each question.

1. Write the missing punctuation in the sentence.

Do you shop at a mall or do you shop on the Internet?

2. Circle the word that should be capitalized in the sentence.

Jeff Bezos started amazon.com in his basement in 1994.

3. Underline the verb in sentence A below.

4. Circle the adverb in sentence A below.

A It quickly grew into a huge Internet business.

5. Write the correct word for the sentence below.

Other companies sell _____ the website, making it even bigger!   (through, threw, though)

6. Circle the correctly spelled word.

enormus

enormous

enourmous

1. Ⓨ Ⓝ

2. Ⓨ Ⓝ

3. Ⓨ Ⓝ

4. Ⓨ Ⓝ

5. Ⓨ Ⓝ

6. Ⓨ Ⓝ

___ / 6
Total

NAME: _____ DATE: _____

DIRECTIONS Read and answer each question.

1. (Y)(N)

2. (Y)(N)

3. (Y)(N)

4. (Y)(N)

5. (Y)(N)

6. (Y)(N)

___ / 6
Total

1. Write the missing punctuation in the sentence.

Francisco takes the train on weekdays and he rides his bike on weekends.

2. Circle the word that should be capitalized in the sentence.

He takes the City metroline to work.

3. Underline the prepositional phrase in sentence A below.

4. Circle the verb in sentence A below.

A He reads the newspaper on the train.

5. Write the correct word for the sentence below.

Do you _____ why he likes to bike?
(now, know, no)

6. Circle the correctly spelled word.

exercise

excercise

exersice

NAME: _____ **DATE:** _____

DIRECTIONS Read and answer each question.

1. Write the missing punctuation in the sentence.

The first subway in New York City opened on October 27 1904.

1. Ⓨ Ⓝ

2. Ⓨ Ⓝ

2. Circle the word that should be capitalized in the sentence.

The oldest subway is in london.

3. Ⓨ Ⓝ

3. Underline the adjective in sentence A below.

4. Ⓨ Ⓝ

4. Circle the verb in sentence A below.

Ⓐ It cost one nickel to ride subway cars.

5. Ⓨ Ⓝ

6. Ⓨ Ⓝ

5. Write the correct word for the sentence below.

Now people have a _____ of transportation.
(choose, choice, chose)

___ / 6
Total

6. Circle the correctly spelled word.

regullar

reguler

regular

NAME: _____ DATE: _____

DIRECTIONS Read and answer each question.

1. (Y)(N)

1. Write the missing punctuation in the sentence.

The earth shook hard around San Francisco on October 17 1989.

2. (Y)(N)

2. Circle the word that should be capitalized in the sentence.

People watching baseball's World series on TV saw it happen.

3. (Y)(N)

3. Underline the conjunction in sentence A below.

4. (Y)(N)

4. Circle the adjective in sentence A below.

5. (Y)(N)

A Freeways fell, and many cars below were crushed.

6. (Y)(N)

___ / 6
Total

5. Write the correct word for the sentence below.

Many people were without power for _____.

(daze, days)

6. Circle the correctly spelled word.

disaster

disester

dissaster

NAME: _____ DATE: _____

DIRECTIONS Read and answer each question.

1. Write the missing punctuation in the sentence.

> Relief gardens, planted during the Great Depression helped feed people.

2. Circle the word that should be capitalized in the sentence.

> Victory gardens were planted during world War II.

3. Underline the verb in sentence A below.

4. Circle the plural noun in sentence A below.

> **A** Now, many people enjoy a community garden.

5. Write the correct word for the sentence below.

> _____ great to have fresh vegetables in the summer.
> (Its, It's)

6. Circle the correctly spelled word.

> locatoin
>
> location
>
> locateon

1. Ⓨ Ⓝ

2. Ⓨ Ⓝ

3. Ⓨ Ⓝ

4. Ⓨ Ⓝ

5. Ⓨ Ⓝ

6. Ⓨ Ⓝ

___ / 6
Total

NAME: _____ **DATE:** _____

DIRECTIONS Read and answer each question.

1. Ⓨ Ⓝ

1. Write the missing punctuation in the sentence.

If you live where there is wind a windmill may be useful.

2. Ⓨ Ⓝ

2. Circle the word that should be capitalized in the sentence.

3. Ⓨ Ⓝ

Some windmills in holland are used to pump up water.

4. Ⓨ Ⓝ

3. Underline the verb in sentence A below.

5. Ⓨ Ⓝ

4. Circle the adjective in sentence A below.

A Many windmills were used for milling grain.

6. Ⓨ Ⓝ

____ / 6
Total

5. Write the correct word for the sentence below.

The blades that turn and catch the wind are called _____.

(sales, sails)

6. Circle the correctly spelled word.

unussual

unusual

unnusual

NAME: _____ **DATE:** _____

DIRECTIONS Read and answer each question.

SCORE

1. Write the missing punctuation in the sentence.

When May 1 comes people usually think about flowers.

2. Circle the word that should be capitalized in the sentence.

known as May Day, it's when people also think about workers.

3. Underline the proper noun in sentence A below.

4. Circle the plural noun in sentence A below.

Ⓐ On May 1, 1886, 400,000 workers went on strike in Chicago.

5. Write the correct word for the sentence below.

The workers wanted the _____ of an eight-hour day.
(right, rite)

6. Circle the correctly spelled word.

factorry

factory

factorie

1. Ⓨ Ⓝ

2. Ⓨ Ⓝ

3. Ⓨ Ⓝ

4. Ⓨ Ⓝ

5. Ⓨ Ⓝ

6. Ⓨ Ⓝ

___ / 6
Total

NAME: _____ **DATE:** _____

SCORE

1. Ⓨ Ⓝ

2. Ⓨ Ⓝ

3. Ⓨ Ⓝ

4. Ⓨ Ⓝ

5. Ⓨ Ⓝ

6. Ⓨ Ⓝ

___ / 6
Total

DIRECTIONS Read and answer each question.

1. Write the missing punctuation in the sentence.

Did you know that people in many countries eat bugs

2. Circle the word that should be capitalized in the sentence.

You might say, "yuck!"

3. Underline the verb in sentence A below.

4. Circle the prepositional phrase in sentence A below.

A Many bugs are good sources of protein.

5. Write the correct word for the sentence below.

Bugs are usually _____, too.
(cheep, cheap)

6. Circle the correctly spelled word.

available

avaleable

avalable

NAME: _____ **DATE:** _____

DIRECTIONS Read and answer each question.

1. Write the missing punctuation in the sentence.

When it wants dinner the cheetah can't be beat.

1. Ⓨ Ⓝ

2. Ⓨ Ⓝ

2. Circle the word that should be capitalized in the sentence.

Found in africa, cheetahs can sprint up to 60 miles (97 kilometers) per hour.

3. Ⓨ Ⓝ

4. Ⓨ Ⓝ

3. Underline the contraction in sentence A below.

4. Circle the pronoun in sentence A below.

5. Ⓨ Ⓝ

Ⓐ They can't keep up that speed for long.

6. Ⓨ Ⓝ

5. Write the correct word for the sentence below.

___ / 6

Total

Once they catch their _____, they hide it from other animals.   (prey, pray)

6. Circle the correctly spelled word.

discovired

discovered

discovvered

NAME: _____ DATE: _____

DIRECTIONS Read and answer each question.

1. Write the missing punctuation in the sentence.

1. Ⓨ Ⓝ

How many pounds of trash do you make each day

2. Ⓨ Ⓝ

2. Circle the word that should be capitalized in the sentence.

3. Ⓨ Ⓝ

People in the United states make about four pounds (two kilograms) of waste each day.

4. Ⓨ Ⓝ

3. Underline the prepositional phrase in sentence A below.

4. Circle the verb in sentence A below.

5. Ⓨ Ⓝ

6. Ⓨ Ⓝ

Ⓐ However, we recycle more now than in the past years.

___ / 6
Total

5. Write the correct word for the sentence below.

Before you _____ something out, try to reuse or recycle it!   (through, throe, throw)

6. Circle the correctly spelled word.

garbige

garbadge

garbage

NAME: _____ **DATE:** _____

DIRECTIONS Read and answer each question.

1. Write the missing punctuation in the sentence.

If it is springtime it may be tornado time.

1. Ⓨ Ⓝ

2. Ⓨ Ⓝ

2. Circle the word that should be capitalized in the sentence.

Tornadoes form a lot in the midwest in the spring.

3. Ⓨ Ⓝ

3. Underline the articles in sentence A below.

4. Ⓨ Ⓝ

4. Circle the nouns in sentence A below.

Ⓐ A tornado looks like a funnel.

5. Ⓨ Ⓝ

6. Ⓨ Ⓝ

5. Write the correct word for the sentence below.

Many people head to the _____ during a tornado.
(seller, cellar)

___ / 6

Total

6. Circle the correctly spelled word.

twister

twistter

twisster

NAME: _____ **DATE:** _____

SCORE

1. Ⓨ Ⓝ

2. Ⓨ Ⓝ

3. Ⓨ Ⓝ

4. Ⓨ Ⓝ

5. Ⓨ Ⓝ

6. Ⓨ Ⓝ

___ / 6
Total

DIRECTIONS Read and answer each question.

1. Write the missing punctuation in the sentence.

If you have read fables you have heard of Aesop.

2. Circle the word that should be capitalized in the sentence.

Some people think he was a slave from ancient greece.

3. Underline the prepositional phrase in sentence A below.

4. Circle the article in sentence A below.

A Others think the fables came from many storytellers.

5. Write the correct word for the sentence below.

Fables often end with a lesson called a _____.
(morale, moral)

6. Circle the correctly spelled word.

publich

publesh

publish

© Shell Education

NAME: _____ **DATE:** _____

DIRECTIONS Read and answer each question.

1. Write the missing punctuation in the sentence.

Some dogs, such as rescue dogs are hardworking.

1. Ⓨ Ⓝ

2. Ⓨ Ⓝ

2. Circle the word that should be capitalized in the sentence.

german shepherds have a good sense of smell.

3. Ⓨ Ⓝ

3. Underline the conjunction in sentence A below.

4. Ⓨ Ⓝ

4. Circle the helping verb in sentence A below.

5. Ⓨ Ⓝ

Ⓐ They are trained to sniff for people buried under snow or rubble.

6. Ⓨ Ⓝ

5. Write the correct word for the sentence below.

___ / 6
Total

They will bark at the _____ when they find someone.
(sight, site)

6. Circle the correctly spelled word.

search

seach

surch

NAME: _____ DATE: _____

SCORE

DIRECTIONS Read and answer each question.

1. Y N

1. Write the missing punctuation in the sentence.

....

After a lot of use rubber tires become scrap.

....

2. Y N

2. Circle the word that should be capitalized in the sentence.

....

3. Y N

In florida, scrap tires were used for an artificial reef.

....

4. Y N

3. Underline the adjectives in sentence A below.

5. Y N

4. Circle the linking verb in sentence A below.

....

A But the tire reefs were a bad idea.

....

6. Y N

5. Write the correct word for the sentence below.

....

___ / 6
Total

_____ scientists are looking for a way to get them out of the ocean.

(Now, Know, No)

....

6. Circle the correctly spelled word.

....

trikiest

trickest

trickiest

....

© Shell Education

NAME: _____ **DATE:** _____

DIRECTIONS Read and answer each question.

1. Write the missing punctuation in the sentence.

In 1975 everyone wanted to own an unusual pet.

2. Circle the word that should be capitalized in the sentence.

Thought up by gary Dahl, the pet was a rock.

3. Underline the verb in sentence A below.

4. Circle the preposition in sentence A below.

A The pet rock came in its own box.

5. Write the correct word for the sentence below.

The training manual said it could _____ tricks, such as sit or play dead.
(dew, do, due)

6. Circle the correctly spelled word.

deccoration

decorration

decoration

1. Ⓨ Ⓝ

2. Ⓨ Ⓝ

3. Ⓨ Ⓝ

4. Ⓨ Ⓝ

5. Ⓨ Ⓝ

6. Ⓨ Ⓝ

___ / 6
Total

NAME: _____ DATE: _____

DIRECTIONS Read and answer each question.

SCORE

1. Ⓨ Ⓝ

2. Ⓨ Ⓝ

3. Ⓨ Ⓝ

4. Ⓨ Ⓝ

5. Ⓨ Ⓝ

6. Ⓨ Ⓝ

___ / 6
Total

1. Write the missing punctuation in the sentence.

If you look closely you can see right through this fish.

2. Circle the word that should be capitalized in the sentence.

The X-ray tetra is found in the Amazon river.

3. Underline the possessive noun in sentence A below.

4. Circle the pronoun in sentence A below.

Ⓐ You can see the fish's backbone through the skin.

5. Write the correct word for the sentence below.

_____ a small fish that lives in groups.
(It's, Its)

6. Circle the correctly spelled word.

aquarium

acquarium

aquareum

NAME: _____ DATE: _____

DIRECTIONS Read and answer each question.

1. Write the missing punctuation in the sentence.

If you eat pancakes you may pour something from a tree on them.

1. Ⓨ Ⓝ

2. Ⓨ Ⓝ

2. Circle the word that should be capitalized in the sentence.

You'll see lots of maple trees in vermont.

3. Ⓨ Ⓝ

3. Underline the plural noun in sentence A below.

4. Ⓨ Ⓝ

4. Circle the conjunction in sentence A below.

Ⓐ Maple trees make sap, and sap is used in syrup.

5. Ⓨ Ⓝ

6. Ⓨ Ⓝ

5. Write the correct word for the sentence below.

___ / 6

Total

To get the sap, bore a _____ in the tree's trunk
(hole, whole)

6. Circle the correctly spelled word.

collecton

colection

collection

NAME: _____ DATE: _____

SCORE

DIRECTIONS Read and answer each question.

1. (Y)(N)

1. Write the missing punctuation in the sentence.

....

The Olympic Games, held every four years are fun to watch.

....

2. (Y)(N)

2. Circle the word that should be capitalized in the sentence.

....

3. (Y)(N)

They started in ancient greece thousands of years ago.

....

4. (Y)(N)

3. Underline the linking verb in sentence A below.

5. (Y)(N)

4. Circle the article in sentence A below.

....

A At first, the games were all races.

6. (Y)(N)

....

5. Write the correct word for the sentence below.

....

___ / 6

Total

The Olympic Games are watched _____ millions of people.

(bye, buy, by)

....

6. Circle the correctly spelled word.

....

victory

victury

victorry

DIRECTIONS Read and answer each question.

1. Write the missing punctuation in the sentence.

1. Ⓨ Ⓝ

Have you ever used a typewriter

2. Ⓨ Ⓝ

2. Circle the word that should be capitalized in the sentence.

Christopher L. sholes invented a practical typewriter in 1873.

3. Ⓨ Ⓝ

3. Underline the article in sentence A below.

4. Ⓨ Ⓝ

4. Circle the pronoun in sentence A below.

5. Ⓨ Ⓝ

A He created a keyboard that is still used today.

6. Ⓨ Ⓝ

5. Write the correct word for the sentence below.

___ / 6
Total

The typewriter's design has gone _____ many changes.
(through, threw)

5. Circle the correctly spelled word.

description

discription

description

NAME: _____ DATE: _____

SCORE

1. Ⓨ Ⓝ

2. Ⓨ Ⓝ

3. Ⓨ Ⓝ

4. Ⓨ Ⓝ

5. Ⓨ Ⓝ

6. Ⓨ Ⓝ

___ / 6
Total

DIRECTIONS   Read and answer each question.

1. Write the missing punctuation in the sentence.

For hundreds of years people have loved coffee.

2. Circle the word that should be capitalized in the sentence.

even during the Civil War, soldiers wanted coffee.

3. Underline the plural noun in sentence A below.

4. Circle the adjective in sentence A below.

Ⓐ   Coffee beans had to be boiled in water.

5. Write the correct word for the sentence below.

The caffeine in coffee _____ to wake you up.
(seems, seams)

6. Circle the correctly spelled word.

available

availible

avalable

© Shell Education

NAME: _____ **DATE:** _____

DIRECTIONS Read and answer each question.

SCORE

1. Write the missing punctuation in the sentence.

If you like to swim you can have fun and stay cool.

1. Ⓨ Ⓝ

2. Circle the word that should be capitalized in the sentence.

Jeremiah and Jenna like to swim at the River city Water Park.

2. Ⓨ Ⓝ

3. Ⓨ Ⓝ

3. Underline the prepositional phrase in sentence A below.

4. Ⓨ Ⓝ

4. Circle the proper noun in sentence A below.

5. Ⓨ Ⓝ

A Jenna likes floating in an inner tube.

6. Ⓨ Ⓝ

5. Write the correct word for the sentence below.

Jeremiah likes floating, but he likes swimming laps, _____.
(two, to, too)

___ / 6
Total

6. Circle the correctly spelled word.

wieghtless

wateless

weightless

NAME: _____ DATE: _____

SCORE

1. Ⓨ Ⓝ

2. Ⓨ Ⓝ

3. Ⓨ Ⓝ

4. Ⓨ Ⓝ

5. Ⓨ Ⓝ

6. Ⓨ Ⓝ

___ / 6
Total

DIRECTIONS Read and answer each question.

1. Write the missing punctuation in the sentence.

....

If you have a big job to do make a plan.

....

2. Circle the word that should be capitalized in the sentence.

....

Students at south Street School planned and planted a big garden.

....

3. Underline the pronoun in sentence A below.

4. Circle the verb in sentence A below.

....

Ⓐ They worked on it in the spring and summer.

....

5. Write the correct word for the sentence below.

....

_____ were lots of vegetables to harvest in the fall.

(They're, Their, There)

....

6. Circle the correctly spelled word.

....

determined

deterrmined

deurmined

....

© Shell Education

NAME: _____ **DATE:** _____

DIRECTIONS Read and answer each question.

1. Write the missing punctuation in the sentence.

If you like beautiful countryside visit Alaska.

1. (Y)(N)

2. Circle the word that should be capitalized in the sentence.

On january 3, 1959, Alaska joined the United States.

2. (Y)(N)

3. (Y)(N)

3. Underline the proper nouns in sentence A below.

4. (Y)(N)

4. Circle the prepositional phrase in sentence A below.

5. (Y)(N)

A Alaska was purchased from Russia.

6. (Y)(N)

5. Write the correct word for the sentence below.

____ / 6
Total

The _____ can be very cold in the winter!
(weather, whether)

6. Circle the correctly spelled word.

glaceir

glacer

glacier

NAME: _____ DATE: _____

SCORE

1. Ⓨ Ⓝ

2. Ⓨ Ⓝ

3. Ⓨ Ⓝ

4. Ⓨ Ⓝ

5. Ⓨ Ⓝ

6. Ⓨ Ⓝ

___ / 6
Total

DIRECTIONS Read and answer each question.

1. Write the missing punctuation in the sentence.

Dr. Seuss wrote many books such as <u>Hop on Pop</u>.

2. Circle the word that should be capitalized in the sentence.

His full name was Theodor Seuss geisel.

3. Underline the plural noun in sentence A below.

4. Circle the verbs in sentence A below.

Ⓐ He wrote and illustrated 44 books.

5. Write the correct word for the sentence below.

His books are loved _____ many people around the world.
(buy, by, bye)

6. Circle the correctly spelled word.

rhyme

rhymn

ryhme

NAME: _____ **DATE:** _____

DIRECTIONS Read and answer each question.

1. Write the missing punctuation in the sentence.

On August 21 1959, the 50th state joined the United States.

2. Circle the word that should be capitalized in the sentence.

Made up of islands, Hawaii is in the Pacific ocean.

3. Underline the prepositions in sentence A below.

4. Circle the linking verb in sentence A below.

Ⓐ The capital is Honolulu on the island of Oahu.

5. Write the correct word for the sentence below.

_____ have lots to do if you visit Hawaii.
(Yule, You, You'll)

6. Circle the correctly spelled word.

volcano

volcanoe

vulcano

1. Ⓨ Ⓝ

2. Ⓨ Ⓝ

3. Ⓨ Ⓝ

4. Ⓨ Ⓝ

5. Ⓨ Ⓝ

6. Ⓨ Ⓝ

___ / 6
Total

NAME: _____ DATE: _____

DIRECTIONS Read and answer each question.

SCORE

1. ⓎⓃ

2. ⓎⓃ

3. ⓎⓃ

4. ⓎⓃ

5. ⓎⓃ

6. ⓎⓃ

___ / 6
Total

1. Write the missing punctuation in the sentence.

Carson likes to take pictures and Mia likes to make movies.

2. Circle the word that should be capitalized in the sentence.

Carson found an old kodak camera in his attic.

3. Underline the prepositional phrase in sentence A below.

4. Circle the adverb in sentence A below.

Ⓐ People can easily take pictures with their cell phones.

5. Write the correct word for the sentence below.

Digital cameras are more _____.
(current, currant)

6. Circle the correctly spelled word.

portraite

portrait

portrate

© Shell Education

NAME: _____ **DATE:** _____

DIRECTIONS Read and answer each question.

1. Write the missing punctuation in the sentence.

From 1861 to 1865 the United States was at war.

1. Ⓨ Ⓝ

2. Circle the word that should be capitalized in the sentence.

The Civil war had many causes, and slavery was one of them.

2. Ⓨ Ⓝ

3. Ⓨ Ⓝ

3. Underline the linking verb in sentence A below.

4. Circle the proper noun in sentence A below.

4. Ⓨ Ⓝ

Ⓐ Abraham Lincoln was the president.

5. Ⓨ Ⓝ

5. Write the correct word for the sentence below.

6. Ⓨ Ⓝ

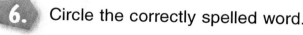

Historians now think more than 700,000 soldiers _____.
(dyed, died, dead)

___ / 6
Total

6. Circle the correctly spelled word.

survant

servent

servant

NAME: _____ DATE: _____

SCORE

DIRECTIONS Read and answer each question.

1. Ⓨ Ⓝ

1. Write the missing punctuation in the sentence.

Do you ever look at the man in the moon

2. Ⓨ Ⓝ

2. Circle the word that should be capitalized in the sentence.

3. Ⓨ Ⓝ

A story from china tells about a toad in the moon.

4. Ⓨ Ⓝ

3. Underline the nouns in sentence A below.

4. Circle the prepositional phrase in sentence A below.

5. Ⓨ Ⓝ

A We do know that the moon is not made of cheese.

6. Ⓨ Ⓝ

5. Write the correct word for the sentence below.

___ / 6
Total

Some people say _____ a woman in the moon.
(they're, theirs, there's)

6. Circle the correctly spelled word.

luner

lunur

lunar

#51169—180 Days of Language

© Shell Education

NAME: _____ **DATE:** _____

DIRECTIONS Read and answer each question.

1. Write the missing punctuation in the sentence.

Did you know that our sun is a star

1. Ⓨ Ⓝ

2. Circle the word that should be capitalized in the sentence.

It's on the outer part of the Milky way galaxy.

2. Ⓨ Ⓝ

3. Ⓨ Ⓝ

3. Underline the article in sentence A below.

4. Ⓨ Ⓝ

4. Circle the linking verb in sentence A below.

Ⓐ The sun is made of layers of gases.

5. Ⓨ Ⓝ

6. Ⓨ Ⓝ

5. Write the correct word for the sentence below.

_____ very far away from Earth.
(Its, It's)

___ / 6
Total

6. Circle the correctly spelled word.

solar

solur

soler

NAME: _____ DATE: _____

SCORE

1. Ⓨ Ⓝ

2. Ⓨ Ⓝ

3. Ⓨ Ⓝ

4. Ⓨ Ⓝ

5. Ⓨ Ⓝ

6. Ⓨ Ⓝ

___ / 6
Total

DIRECTIONS Read and answer each question.

1. Write the missing punctuation in the sentence.

What is your favorite summer holiday

2. Circle the word that should be capitalized in the sentence.

The 4th of july celebrates America's independence.

3. Underline the conjunction in sentence A below.

4. Circle the adjectives in sentence A below.

A Many people enjoy going to picnics, fireworks, and ball games.

5. Write the correct word for the sentence below.

Some fireworks light up the sky like _____.
(lightening, lightning)

6. Circle the correctly spelled word.

selabration

celebration

celabration

© Shell Education

NAME: _____ **DATE:** _____

DIRECTIONS Read and answer each question.

1. Write the missing punctuation in the sentence.

After going to college Ramon knows what he wants to do.

1. Ⓨ Ⓝ

2. Circle the word that should be capitalized in the sentence.

Ramon wants to be a conductor on an amtrak train.

2. Ⓨ Ⓝ

3. Ⓨ Ⓝ

3. Underline the verbs in sentence A below.

4. Ⓨ Ⓝ

4. Circle the adjective in sentence A below.

5. Ⓨ Ⓝ

Ⓐ He likes traveling and seeing new places.

6. Ⓨ Ⓝ

5. Write the correct word for the sentence below.

He even likes to help people _____ their luggage.
(load, lode)

___ / 6
Total

6. Circle the correctly spelled word.

enginere

engineir

engineer

© Shell Education

NAME: _____ **DATE:** _____

SCORE

1. Ⓨ Ⓝ

2. Ⓨ Ⓝ

3. Ⓨ Ⓝ

4. Ⓨ Ⓝ

5. Ⓨ Ⓝ

6. Ⓨ Ⓝ

___ / 6
Total

DIRECTIONS Read and answer each question.

1. Write the missing punctuation in the sentence.

After getting your allowance what do you do next?

2. Circle the word that should be capitalized in the sentence.

When he was seven, Ben franklin bought a toy whistle.

3. Underline the proper noun in sentence A below.

4. Circle the article in sentence A below.

Ⓐ Franklin learned later that he paid too much for the whistle.

5. Write the correct word for the sentence below.

He had learned not to pay _____ much for anything.
(to, too, two)

6. Circle the correctly spelled word.

exampil

exampel

example

NAME: _____ **DATE:** _____

DIRECTIONS Read and answer each question.

1. Write the missing punctuation in the sentence.

On June 25, 1894 a young mother climbed on her bike and rode away.

1. Ⓨ Ⓝ

2. Ⓨ Ⓝ

2. Circle the word that should be capitalized in the sentence.

Leaving boston, Annie Londonderry started biking around the world.

3. Ⓨ Ⓝ

3. Underline the conjunction in sentence A below.

4. Ⓨ Ⓝ

4. Circle the possessive pronoun in sentence A below.

5. Ⓨ Ⓝ

Ⓐ Her ride lasted 15 months, but she made it!

6. Ⓨ Ⓝ

5. Write the correct word for the sentence below.

She earned her way by delivering _____ on her bike.
(ads, adds, adze)

___ / 6
Total

6. Circle the correctly spelled word.

determuned

determined

determained

NAME: _____ DATE: _____

DIRECTIONS Read and answer each question.

1. Y N

1. Write the missing punctuation in the sentence.

In 1985 kids could buy the first box of 64 crayons.

2. Y N

2. Circle the word that should be capitalized in the sentence.

3. Y N

the crayon pack had 13 shades of blue in it.

4. Y N

3. Underline the pronoun in sentence A below.

5. Y N

4. Circle the prepositional phrase in sentence A below.

A Now, you can even buy crayons with glitter!

6. Y N

5. Write the correct word for the sentence below.

___ / 6
Total

It's always fun to _____ a new box of crayons.
(choose, choice, chose)

6. Circle the correctly spelled word.

arttist

artest

artist

© Shell Education

NAME: _____ DATE: _____

DIRECTIONS Read and answer each question.

1. Write the missing punctuation in the sentence.

When introduced in 1963 zip codes first had five numbers.

2. Circle the word that should be capitalized in the sentence.

you may know that zip stands for zone improvement plan.

3. Underline the adjective in sentence A below.

4. Circle the preposition in sentence A below.

A Some people disliked using them at first.

5. Write the correct word for the sentence below.

Now, the Post Office hopes you'll write a nine-number code on your

_____.

(mail, male)

6. Circle the correctly spelled word.

persuade

persaude

persuad

1. Ⓨ Ⓝ

2. Ⓨ Ⓝ

3. Ⓨ Ⓝ

4. Ⓨ Ⓝ

5. Ⓨ Ⓝ

6. Ⓨ Ⓝ

___ / 6
Total

NAME: _____ **DATE:** _____

SCORE

1. (Y)(N)

2. (Y)(N)

3. (Y)(N)

4. (Y)(N)

5. (Y)(N)

6. (Y)(N)

___ / 6
Total

DIRECTIONS Read and answer each question.

1. Write the missing punctuation in the sentence.

In 1982 a man attached 42 weather balloons to a lawn chair.

2. Circle the word that should be capitalized in the sentence.

Larry Walters, later known as Lawn chair Walters, wanted to fly.

3. Underline the plural noun in sentence A below.

4. Circle the proper noun in sentence A below.

A   Filled with helium, the balloons launched Walters into the air.

5. Write the correct word for the sentence below.

He flew higher than planned, and he was _____ for
his flight.   (find, fine, fined)

6. Circle the correctly spelled word.

capeble

capable

capeable

NAME: _____ **DATE:** _____

DIRECTIONS Read and answer each question.

1. Write the missing punctuation in the sentence.

At the age of 51 Joshua Slocum left the Boston Harbor alone.

1. Ⓨ Ⓝ

2. Ⓨ Ⓝ

2. Circle the word that should be capitalized in the sentence.

It was April 24, 1895, and he was in a tiny sloop, *spray*.

3. Ⓨ Ⓝ

3. Underline the verb in sentence A below.

4. Ⓨ Ⓝ

4. Circle the pronoun in sentence A below.

5. Ⓨ Ⓝ

Ⓐ He returned more than three years later.

6. Ⓨ Ⓝ

5. Write the correct word for the sentence below.

___ / 6
Total

His round-the-world voyage was a major _____.
(feet, feat)

6. Circle the correctly spelled word.

exampile

example

exampel

NAME: _____ DATE: _____

SCORE

1. Ⓨ Ⓝ

2. Ⓨ Ⓝ

3. Ⓨ Ⓝ

4. Ⓨ Ⓝ

5. Ⓨ Ⓝ

6. Ⓨ Ⓝ

___ / 6
Total

DIRECTIONS Read and answer each question.

1. Write the missing punctuation in the sentence.

When summer comes be sure to keep cool.

2. Circle the word that should be capitalized in the sentence.

In Death valley, California, the temperature once rose to 134°F (57°C)!

3. Underline the adverb in sentence A below.

4. Circle the adjective in sentence A below.

A Hot weather can quickly make you feel sick.

5. Write the correct word for the sentence below.

It can be really hot in a _____.
(desert, dessert)

6. Circle the correctly spelled word.

wilderness

wildeness

wildurness

© Shell Education

NAME: _____ **DATE:** _____

DIRECTIONS Read and answer each question.

SCORE

1. Write the missing punctuation in the sentence.

Andy, a polar bear found it hard to keep cool at the zoo.

1. Ⓨ Ⓝ

2. Circle the word that should be capitalized in the sentence.

He would get too hot at the Atlanta zoo.

2. Ⓨ Ⓝ

3. Ⓨ Ⓝ

3. Underline the verb in sentence A below.

4. Ⓨ Ⓝ

4. Circle the proper noun in sentence A below.

5. Ⓨ Ⓝ

A A company kindly gave Andy his own ice machine.

6. Ⓨ Ⓝ

5. Write the correct word for the sentence below.

___ / 6

Total

Andy could _____ the heat for the rest of his life.
(beat, beet)

6. Circle the correctly spelled word.

refrigeratur

refrigerater

refrigerator

NAME: _____ DATE: _____

SCORE

DIRECTIONS Read and answer each question.

1. Ⓨ Ⓝ

2. Ⓨ Ⓝ

3. Ⓨ Ⓝ

4. Ⓨ Ⓝ

5. Ⓨ Ⓝ

6. Ⓨ Ⓝ

___ / 6
Total

1. Write the missing punctuation in the sentence.

How would you like to be a treasure hunter

2. Circle the word that should be capitalized in the sentence.

Mel Fisher found a sunken spanish ship in 1985.

3. Underline the plural noun in sentence A below.

4. Circle the conjunction in sentence A below.

A The ship held 47 tons of gold and silver.

5. Write the correct word for the sentence below.

Fisher had searched for 16 years before finding _____
the treasure was.   (where, were, we're)

6. Circle the correctly spelled word.

expolre

exploar

explore

© Shell Education

NAME: _____ **DATE:** _____

DIRECTIONS	Read and answer each question.

1. Write the missing punctuation in the sentence.

In July and August people may say it's the dog days of summer.

1. Ⓨ Ⓝ

2. Ⓨ Ⓝ

2. Circle the word that should be capitalized in the sentence.

This phrase is based on sirius, which is also known as the Dog Star.

3. Ⓨ Ⓝ

3. Underline the plural common noun in sentence A below.

4. Ⓨ Ⓝ

4. Circle the plural proper noun in sentence A below.

5. Ⓨ Ⓝ

A The Romans thought this bright star caused the hot days.

6. Ⓨ Ⓝ

5. Write the correct word for the sentence below.

___ / 6

Total

People like being _____ on really hot days.
(idol, idyll, idle)

6. Circle the correctly spelled word.

relax

rellax

reelax

ANSWER KEY

Day 1

1. "I just read the greatest book!" said Maria.
2. The title of Maria's book was **Untamed** by Shelly Fergus.
3. bought
4. Maria
5. too
6. library

Day 2

1. Jack, Nita, and Marty ran to the bus**.**
2. They always ride on the **Pleasantville** bus at 3:30.
3. happily
4. friends, bus
5. They're
6. another

Day 3

1. Are you going to the county fair this Saturday**?**
2. **Mrs.** Kim, Jin, and her brother are taking me.
3. I
4. fast
5. off
6. amuse

Day 4

1. Mina**'s** brother loves going to the haunted house in October.
2. "Can we go there today?" **Mina's** brother asked,
3. They
4. a, long
5. quite
6. ghost

Day 5

1. Ali looked at clock and shouted, "I'm late!"
2. **Hunter** was waiting for Ali outside.
3. bikes
4. to the zoo
5. Which
6. daughter

Day 6

1. "Would you like to go to the animal rescue**?**" Mila asked Raisa.
2. Let's go to the store on **Main** Street.
3. Mila, Raisa
4. stopped
5. loose
6. raccoon

Day 7

1. Ethan's favorite places are rivers**,** lakes, and creeks.
2. Lyla and Ethan had a snack by **Sand Hill** River.
3. by
4. It
5. through
6. scratch

Day 8

1. Owen said, "I'm getting tired. I think it's time to go home.**"**
2. **Cole** said, "Maybe my dad can pick us up."
3. and
4. waited
5. their
6. luckily

Day 9

1. **"**Shall we pick up a pizza for dinner tonight?" Riku's dad asked.
2. "That would be great, **Mr.** Sato," Sami replied.
3. a, large
4. hungrily
5. scent
6. grateful

Day 10

1. "What shall we do tomorrow**?**" Kala asked.
2. "It's hard to think about that when **I'm** this tired," said Dominic.
3. Dad
4. You
5. sighed
6. peaceful

Day 11

1. Yuki read a book about Susan B**.** Anthony.
2. She was the first woman to have her picture on an **American** coin.
3. fought
4. for women's rights
5. knew
6. ability

Day 12

1. Amin likes to read books about writers**.**
2. He read a book about Louisa **May** Alcott.
3. famous, Little
4. Her
5. meet
6. author

© Shell Education

ANSWER KEY *(cont.)*

Day 13
1. A famous ocean liner sank on April 15**,** 1912.
2. It was named the RMS *Titanic.*
3. ship, iceberg, water
4. struck, sank
5. main
6. beneath

Day 14
1. Do you have a bicycle**?**
2. The Schwinn **Bicycle** Company was founded in 1895.
3. produced
4. in
5. weighed
6. further

Day 15
1. Would you like to travel on a train**,** a ship, or a plane?
2. You can travel on any of them from San **Francisco.**
3. San Francisco
4. is
5. weather
6. purpose

Day 16
1. Neo likes to swim**,** and Ellie likes to ride bikes.
2. They decided to bike to the **Oakdale** swimming pool.
3. ribbons, bikes
4. on
5. sale
6. persuade

Day 17
1. Have you been to New York City**,** New York?
2. Some people think it is the most exciting city in the **United** States.
3. You
4. Broadway
5. There
6. popular

Day 18
1. What is your favorite city**?**
2. Is it in the **United** States or another country?
3. like
4. Many people
5. your
6. seize

Day 19
1. The first snowboard was invented in Muskegon**,** Michigan.
2. It was invented by **Sherman** Poppen.
3. *Snurfer*
4. and
5. you
6. slippery

Day 20
1. What did you have for dinner last night**?**
2. Roi's favorite restaurant is Big Joe's **Diner.**
3. orders
4. Roi
5. They're
6. spoiled

Day 21
1. Jasmine's best friend is Morgan**.**
2. They love to watch the *Star Wars* movies.
3. took
4. her
5. It's
6. believable

Day 22
1. "Stop, thief**!** " cried the giant to Jack.
2. But **Jack** hung onto the harp and climbed down the beanstalk.
3. the, huge
4. He
5. climb
6. heavy

Day 23
1. When she was young, my mother's favorite book was Peter Pan.
2. Peter Pan was written by J. M. **Barrie.**
3. resembles
4. Tinker Bell
5. fairy
6. magical

Day 24
1. "Let's take out the sailboat at 2:00 P.M.," Finn said.
2. Finn's sailboat is called the *Sharkfin.*
3. likes
4. beautiful
5. seas
6. harbor

ANSWER KEY *(cont.)*

Day 25
1. African elephants can be found in Kenya**,** Africa.
2. They can also be found in **South** Africa.
3. elephants, animals
4. and
5. prey
6. weigh

Day 26
1. Some people live in houses**,** and some people live in condos.
2. There's an apartment building in New York City Spruce **Street**.
3. you
4. above
5. stare
6. furniture

Day 27
1. Years ago**,** people did most of their cooking over fires.
2. You can still cook over a fire at Morris State **Park**.
3. you
4. the, black
5. would
6. knives

Day 28
1. "Let's go to see the parade tomorrow," said Elijah.
2. The parade starts at **River** Street Park.
3. Elijah
4. decorative, the, best, the
5. whether
6. neighbor

Day 29
1. Many art museums have artwork by Claude Monet**.**
2. Monet was born in **Paris**, France, in 1840.
3. painted, using
4. in
5. style
6. flower

Day 30
1. Have you ever seen a Maine Coon cat**?**
2. Some people think Captain **Charles** Coon brought these cats to America.
3. these, long-haired
4. Others, cats, raccoons
5. main
6. loyal

Day 31
1. Would you like to get paid for taking a walk**?**
2. Teens who work at the Dog **Walk** Company do!
3. in
4. They
5. may be
6. beast

Day 32
1. Your mouth includes a tongue, a roof, a base, teeth, and lips**.**
2. Dr. **Perez** is an orthodontist in the city.
3. my
4. made
5. peer
6. swallow

Day 33
1. The Gateway Arch is in St. Louis**,** Missouri.
2. The capital of Missouri is Jefferson **City**.
3. train, city
4. Kira, Lina
5. sales
6. governor

Day 34
1. Watch out for the car**!**
2. **Henry Ford** first produced the popular **Ford** Model T car in 1908.
3. affordable
4. cars
5. buy
6. caution

Day 35
1. Bo**,** fetch the stick!
2. Bo loves to play fetch with **Jaden**.
3. Bo, Australia
4. a, huge
5. very
6. worried

Day 36
1. "Let's go see the sharks at the aquarium," Laila said.
2. The Monterey **Aquarium** has a great white shark in a tank.
3. eat
4. sea, bony, other
5. reign
6. hurried

© Shell Education

ANSWER KEY *(cont.)*

Day 37

1. Rio wanted to go on a treasure hunt**,** but Mai wanted to play inside.
2. "Let's pretend I'm **Blackbeard**," Rio said.
3. about
4. a
5. their
6. disagree

Day 38

1. The Abraham Lincoln Presidential Library is in Springfield**,** Illinois.
2. Springfield is near Clear **Lake**.
3. is
4. Springfield, Chicago
5. your
6. surface

Day 39

1. Would you like to go on an ocean liner**?**
2. One of the longest cruise ships is called the *Oasis of the Seas*.
3. work
4. on
5. weighs
6. staircase

Day 40

1. Have you visited our nation's capital city**?**
2. Washington, D.C., is on the Potomac **River**.
3. museums
4. Capitol
5. sight
6. preserve

Day 41

1. "Clang, clang, clang," went the trolley.
2. Those are words from "The **Trolley** Song."
3. in, *in*
4. Judy Garland, *Meet Me in St. Louis*
5. quite
6. perform

Day 42

1. The Air Force Academy is in Colorado Springs**,** Colorado.
2. Students are members of the **Air Force**.
3. and
4. Students
5. too
6. general

Day 43

1. The *Viking 1* spacecraft was launched on August 20**,** 1975.
2. The spacecraft took eleven months to get to **Mars**.
3. searched
4. The
5. human
6. voyage

Day 44

1. Have you ever visited a cemetery**?**
2. Boothill Graveyard is in **Tombstone**, Arizona.
3. Many
4. were
5. for
6. countries

Day 45

1. If you drive in New England**,** you might go on a famous road.
2. The Boston **Post** Road began as trails before the colonists came.
3. It's
4. or
5. route
6. private

Day 46

1. Beijing, China, is the biggest city in the world.
2. Beijing used to be called **Peking**.
3. Many Beijing visitors
4. tour
5. off
6. bridge

Day 47

1. If you lived years ago**,** your chewing gum came from a tree.
2. **American** Indians peeled off the bark and scraped off the sticky part.
3. was
4. and
5. choose
6. smooth

Day 48

1. Did you know that you can erase with a dry crust of bread**?**
2. Edward **Naime** picked up some rubber by mistake and began erasing.
3. He
4. discovered, worked
5. sell
6. achieve

ANSWER KEY (cont.)

Day 49

1. Colton's favorite sport is football.
2. He dreams of playing for the Denver **Broncos** when he grows up.
3. field
4. Colton
5. foul
6. guard

Day 50

1. There is nothing better than a clear autumn day**.**
2. The best time to look at colorful leaves is in **October**.
3. We
4. long, the
5. through
6. steady

Day 51

1. It's been more than 100 years since the ballpoint pen was invented.
2. Laszlo **Biro**, a journalist, noticed how newspaper ink dried quickly.
3. was
4. a
5. perfect
6. relief

Day 52

1. Nita begins every day by writing in her journal**.**
2. She likes to buy journals at Barton's **Books** and Magazines.
3. but
4. doesn't
5. You'll
6. feature

Day 53

1. Many people celebrate New Year's Eve on Dec**.** 31.
2. Football games are popular on New Year's **Day**.
3. with gifts
4. celebrate
5. vary
6. receive

Day 54

1. Smokey Bear says, "Only YOU can prevent forest fires!"
2. The United States Forest **Service** created Smokey.
3. a, big
4. Wildfires
5. pair
6. avoid

Day 55

1. "Let**'**s go camping this weekend," Mom said.
2. "Will you get out the tent, **Dad**?" Mom asked.
3. and
4. Lev
5. boulder
6. disease

Day 56

1. In 1869**,** Wyoming gave women the right to vote.
2. There had been no act of **Congress** to allow women to vote.
3. Wyoming
4. Women, years
5. women
6. genius

Day 57

1. Sarita asked, "Would you help me write a play**?**"
2. They called the play *Bunny's Basket*.
3. on
4. kids
5. scene
6. already

Day 58

1. Chi moved to the United States from Hanoi, Vietnam.
2. Chi likes living in **Bridgeway**.
3. and
4. misses
5. writes
6. routine

Day 59

1. Did you ever wonder how the sandwich got its name**?**
2. Long ago, an earl in **England** stuffed some meat between two pieces of bread.
3. the, delicious, the
4. named
5. while
6. delicious

Day 60

1. "Let's get some ice cream**,**" Grandpa said.
2. "We can go to the sundae shop," **Gus** said.
3. on a cone
4. Gus
5. too
6. prefer

© Shell Education

ANSWER KEY (cont.)

Day 61
1. America's first roller coaster held 10 people in one car.
2. It opened in 1884 in Coney **Island**, New York.
3. for a nickel
4. could ride
5. turns
6. amount

Day 62
1. Theodore Roosevelt, our 26th president**,** loved to hunt.
2. He was hunting in **Mississippi**, and he came upon an old bear.
3. the, old
4. Roosevelt
5. known
6. lovable

Day 63
1. Desta likes to paint with oil**,** and Jude likes to use colored chalk.
2. Desta likes to copy famous **French** artists.
3. because
4. it's
5. shown
6. ugliest

Day 64
1. How much would you pay for a circus elephant**?**
2. P. T. **Barnum** paid $10,000 for **Jumbo** the elephant.
3. at the shoulders
4. Jumbo
5. weighed
6. addition

Day 65
1. "It's a great day for baseball!" Jeremy said.
2. You can learn a lot about baseball in **Cooperstown**, New York.
3. is
4. The
5. team
6. bounced

Day 66
1. In 1903**,** the first phone cable was laid in the Pacific Ocean.
2. The cable linked Honolulu and **San** Francisco.
3. a, an, ocean
4. but
5. cell
6. connected

Day 67
1. It's hard to have a cold.
2. Most people in the United **States** catch colds in the fall and winter.
3. in a year
4. catch
5. There's
6. power

Day 68
1. "Guess what**!**" cried Cerillo. "We're going to see the giraffes."
2. The tallest giraffe in the world was **George**.
3. England
4. lived
5. peel
6. dislike

Day 69
1. Nina, Marie, Chan, and Kim went on a scavenger hunt**.**
2. They could stop at any house on Lathrop **Lane**.
3. was
4. on the list
5. piece
6. burden

Day 70
1. The first U.S. hot-air balloon ride was in 1793.
2. A man and his dog lifted up over **Philadelphia**.
3. landed
4. safely
5. lightning
6. orbit

Day 71
1. Flying in a jet can be fun**,** and it can also be tiring.
2. Some airlines, such as ATA **Airlines**, have closed.
3. for years
4. train, fly
5. plane
6. motion

Day 72
1. In 1898**,** a quart of milk cost six cents.
2. Shop girls in **Boston** made about $5.00 a week.
3. earned
4. a
5. hire
6. labor

ANSWER KEY (cont.)

Day 73
1. Have you ever been in a building with five sides**?**
2. The **Pentagon** is a huge office building in Washington, D.C.
3. and
4. It, it
5. feet
6. answer

Day 74
1. "We'll go roller skating tomorrow," Pieter said.
2. "Let's go to the roller rink," **Dom** said.
3. shout
4. in the rink
5. flew
6. order

Day 75
1. The narwhal, which is a type of whale**,** has a very long tooth.
2. Narwhals live in the coastal waters of the **Arctic** Ocean.
3. grows
4. male's
5. through
6. column

Day 76
1. The female orangutan, an ape, is a great mom.
2. Female orangutans are found in Sumatra and **Borneo**.
3. stay
4. or
5. their
6. calendar

Day 77
1. Elizabeth Blackwell graduated from college on January 23**,** 1849.
2. She graduated from Geneva Medical **College**.
3. United States
4. was
5. bow
6. director

Day 78
1. To stay healthy**,** you need to drink plenty of water.
2. Planet **Earth** has water in, on, and above it.
3. can't
4. everywhere
5. seas
6. glisten

Day 79
1. Do you think the dental drill is a new invention**?**
2. George **Green** invented it more than 150 years ago.
3. decayed
4. Dentists, teeth
5. than
6. difficult

Day 80
1. Ham, a chimpanzee**,** flew into space in a rocket.
2. He was born in **Cameroon** in 1957.
3. for his flight
4. and
5. safe
6. reason

Day 81
1. When you go to the airport**,** do you walk on a moving sidewalk?
2. The first one at an airport was at Love **Field** in Dallas, Texas.
3. was
4. of the walkway
5. break
6. elevator

Day 82
1. Eliana's favorite subject is math.
2. The class is taught by **Mr.** Petersen.
3. math
4. competed
5. won
6. support

Day 83
1. "What is your favorite comic strip**?**" Quinn asked.
2. "I like **Peanuts**," Declan said. "Charlie Brown is funny."
3. drew
4. Charles M. Schulz
5. born
6. cartoon

Day 84
1. If you want to be an artist**,** you must practice a lot.
2. That advice comes from **Tomie** dePaola.
3. is
4. Mr. dePaola's
5. course
6. patient

© Shell Education

ANSWER KEY (cont.)

Day 85
1. If you know how to count to 26**,** you can write in code.
2. **Give** each letter of the alphabet a number.
3. write
4. a
5. symbols
6. invent

Day 86
1. Although blinded at age three**,** Louis Braille became famous.
2. Louis **Braille** made a system of bumps for letters.
3. With this system
4. blind
5. soar
6. succeed

Day 87
1. After the Civil War**,** Louisa May Alcott wrote <u>Little Women</u>.
2. During the war, she helped as a nurse in **Washington**, D.C.
3. soldiers
4. More than 250,000 Civil War soldiers
5. stake
6. dangerous

Day 88
1. Pigs can be taught to fetch, sit, and spin in a circle**.**
2. You may know of **Babe**, Wilbur, or Olivia.
3. in a show
4. pigs
5. patience
6. discover

Day 89
1. Born in France**,** Charles Perrault wrote many fairy tales.
2. He wasn't the only person to write about the character **Cinderella**.
3. different
4. are, marry
5. tale
6. pattern

Day 90
1. Martin Luther King Jr. was born in 1928.
2. We celebrate his birthday on the third **Monday** of January.
3. speeches
4. gave
5. rights
6. important

Day 91
1. Cats come in all kinds of patterns**,** such as calico, tabby, and solid.
2. José likes all of his cats, but he likes **Mittens** the most.
3. Boots
4. except for three white paws
5. so
6. disobey

Day 92
1. In 1595**,** one of the first wheelchairs was made.
2. It was made for **King** Phillip II of Spain.
3. invalid's
4. wheelchair
5. then
6. protect

Day 93
1. Lloyd Alexander, a famous writer**,** said he rewrites a lot.
2. One book, <u>The High King</u>, won the Newbery **Medal**.
3. I've
4. Alexander
5. seems
6. energy

Day 94
1. In the 1700s, a shoemaker's son ran off to sea.
2. He fought with a ship's captain and was left on Mas a **Tierra** Island.
3. Alexander
4. after nearly five years
5. based
6. distort

Day 95
1. On February 2, everyone's eyes are on a groundhog.
2. People are encouraged to watch the sky, too, on Groundhog **Day**.
3. and
4. groundhog
5. hole
6. scout

Day 96
1. "Hurry up**!**" Mila yelled.
2. Mila didn't want to be late for the Veterans **Day** parade.
3. served
4. in
5. passed
6. excellent

ANSWER KEY *(cont.)*

Day 97

1. Do you own two, three, or more pairs of shoes**?**
2. During **World** War II, there was a ration on shoes.
3. could
4. People
5. soles
6. interest

Day 98

1. In 1908**,** a penny could buy a lot.
2. You could mail a letter anywhere in the United **States** for a penny.
3. parents
4. Ask, cost
5. cent
6. brought

Day 99

1. "Do you pay attention to what you eat**?**" Ms**.** Tomez asked.
2. "Most of us don't," **Ms**. Tomez said.
3. you'll
4. and
5. choose
6. plentiful

Day 100

1. When you go to the zoo**,** what animals do you visit?
2. The **African** lion is called a "vulnerable" lion.
3. in danger
4. lions
5. Too
6. tractor

Day 101

1. We could go to a movie**,** but I prefer bowling.
2. We could use a coupon for a free game at Joe's **Lanes**.
3. His
4. has
5. roll
6. nuisance

Day 102

1. Wait**. (or !)** I want to try to win a prize!
2. The man at the booth handed **Dad** a baseball.
3. at the bottles
4. pitched
5. won
6. equal

Day 103

1. Do you know what you can find in Wyoming, Montana, and Idaho**?**
2. You can visit Yellowstone National **Park** there.
3. animals
4. Don't
5. bear
6. mound

Day 104

1. In 1853**,** three brothers quit their jobs.
2. They started a piano company called Steinway & **Sons**.
3. pianos
4. the
5. Their
6. pedal

Day 105

1. Washington Irving, born in 1783**,** was a writer.
2. Irving wrote about a man called Rip **Van** Winkle.
3. for
4. Rip
5. do
6. breathe

Day 106

1. "Let's plant a tree for Arbor Day**,**" Malia said.
2. The first Arbor Day, in 1872, was in **Nebraska**.
3. plant
4. Arbor Day
5. It's
6. nature

Day 107

1. If you live in New York City**,** you may call this game *Potsy*.
2. Hopscotch is called *escargot* in **France**, which means "snail."
3. or
4. Don't
5. piece
6. object

Day 108

1. Do you ever look in the attic for old or hidden things**?**
2. You might want to visit Mr. Topper's Treasure **Chest**.
3. and
4. You'll
5. sale
6. cellar

ANSWER KEY *(cont.)*

Day 109

1. In 1997**,** a boa constrictor died at over 40 years old.
2. The boa, named Popeye, lived at the Philadelphia **Zoo**.
3. live
4. boa constrictors, years
5. prey
6. motive

Day 110

1. "Chocolate is my favorite treat," said Tanesha**.**
2. "I visited **Hershey**, Pennsylvania, once," said Ben.
3. from the factory
4. You
5. dessert
6. scent

Day 111

1. Do you use ice skates, in-line skates, or roller skates**?**
2. Skates were used in **Holland** hundreds of years ago.
3. Dutchmen
4. attached, could skate
5. steel
6. scissors

Day 112

1. An Easter Egg Roll was held by President Rutherford B. Hayes.
2. It was held at the **White** House in 1878.
3. the
4. Easter
5. Would
6. collection

Day 113

1. For decades**,** many people have worried about whales.
2. World Whale **Day** began in 1975.
3. for food
4. mammals
5. die
6. ocean

Day 114

1. On May 5**,** 1961, the first American entered outer space.
2. Alan **Shepard** shot into space as part of the Mercury Project.
3. miles
4. of
5. flew
6. horizon

Day 115

1. A coffin may be made of wood**,** but some are made of gold.
2. In ancient **Egypt**, a king's coffin might be covered with gold.
3. King Tut
4. had
5. wore
6. death

Day 116

1. Railroads built on dirt roads have been around for a long time**.**
2. In the 1700s, **Europeans** began to use iron rails.
3. were
4. the
5. made
6. district

Day 117

1. How far could you drive on three gallons of gas**?**
2. **That's** how much gas people got for a week during World War II.
3. during
4. Sugar and coffee
5. by
6. afford

Day 118

1. You don't have to be Irish to celebrate St**.** Patrick's Day.
2. In Chicago, the Chicago **River** is dyed green.
3. In 1962
4. the, a
5. dye
6. weave

Day 119

1. Sol likes to grow pumpkins**,** and he likes carrots, too.
2. He entered his pumpkin in a contest at the County **Fair**.
3. Biggest County Pumpkin
4. He, his
5. weighs
6. except

Day 120

1. Some frogs jump really high**,** and some frogs jump really far.
2. One frog in **South** Africa was in a frog derby.
3. Santjie
4. and
5. It's
6. busiest

ANSWER KEY *(cont.)*

Day 121
1. Zoe, who is going to the theater**,** asked her friends to come, too.
2. They want to see Clara perform in *Annie*.
3. for the opening curtain
4. don't
5. rode
6. remember

Day 122
1. Jane Yolen was born on February 11**,** 1939.
2. Many young readers love her Commander **Toad** series.
3. at age 22
4. Yolen
5. writes
6. expert

Day 123
1. If you could fly anywhere on your birthday**,** where would you go?
2. Would you fly to Paris, **Rome**, or London?
3. can't
4. you
5. meet
6. distant

Day 124
1. If you have tennis shoes**,** you probably have aglets.
2. The modern shoestring was invented in **England** in 1790.
3. at, of
4. An aglet
5. through
6. buckle

Day 125
1. "Write what you know**,**" writers often say.
2. **However**, you must use your imagination to write about aliens.
3. My, favorite
4. books, aliens
5. four
6. portion

Day 126
1. "My dog ate my homework**"** used to be a common excuse.
2. Now, kids can say, "**My** computer crashed."
3. one, backup
4. It's
5. bytes
6. foolish

Day 127
1. Mark Twain, who wrote <u>The Adventures of Tom Sawyer</u>**,** loved cats.
2. He named one of them Stray **Kit**.
3. owned
4. Twain's
5. bored
6. porch

Day 128
1. Have you heard of Pecos Bill, Widow-Maker**,** and Slue-Foot Sue?
2. Pecos Bill first saw Sue riding a catfish down the Rio **Grande**.
3. and
4. Bill's
5. thrown
6. probably

Day 129
1. It's time to sign up for the spelling bee," Mr**.** Lucero announced.
2. "It's sponsored by the newspaper *City News*," he added.
3. spell, define
4. at this year's contest
5. flair
6. misspelled

Day 130
1. "Look**!** There's a covey of quail outside!" Alma cried.
2. Quail sometimes sound like they are saying, "**Chicago**."
3. Quail, baths
4. dust
5. burrow
6. hatch

Day 131
1. During the mid-1800s, Harriet Tubman helped many slaves escape.
2. The Underground **Railroad** was not a real railroad.
3. People, slaves
4. and
5. site
6. dangerous

Day 132
1. You may not know the name Andrew Lang**,** but you have probably read his work.
2. He collected fairy tales, starting with <u>The Blue Fairy **Book**.</u>
3. for all the titles
4. He
5. know
6. argued

© Shell Education

ANSWER KEY *(cont.)*

Day 133
1. Do you like reading book series such as Harry Potter**?**
2. The Chronicles of **Narnia** is also a great book series.
3. wait
4. Readers, books
5. There's
6. favorite

Day 134
1. During the Great Depression, a man invented a new board game.
2. He sold the game to **Macy's** department store.
3. have played
4. You
5. great
6. brain

Day 135
1. In 1828, the first American dictionary was published.
2. Noah **Webster** spent 22 years writing it.
3. computers
4. his
5. Would
6. rough

Day 136
1. If you want to run in the biggest race, go to the Big Apple.
2. More than 40,000 people race in the New York **City** Marathon.
3. for 26.2 miles
4. You'll
5. feat
6. position

Day 137
1. When you want water, do you turn on a faucet?
2. In parts of **Africa**, women and children haul water in jugs.
3. for hours, with their heavy jugs
4. their
5. desert
6. trouble

Day 138
1. If you like dog stories, be sure to read <u>Old Yeller.</u>
2. It was written by **Fred Gipson** and was a Newbery Honor book.
3. to the book
4. and
5. lesson
6. several

Day 139
1. The first car built by Henry Ford was finished on June 4, 1896.
2. It was built in a shed in **Detroit**, and there was a problem.
3. doors
4. on
5. their
6. difficulty

Day 140
1. Do you shop at a mall, or do you shop on the Internet?
2. Jeff Bezos started **Amazon**.com in his basement in 1994.
3. grew
4. quickly
5. through
6. enormous

Day 141
1. Francisco takes the train on weekdays, and he rides his bike on weekends.
2. He takes the City **Metroline** to work.
3. on the train
4. reads
5. know
6. exercise

Day 142
1. The first subway in New York City opened on October 27, 1904.
2. The oldest subway is in **London**.
3. one, subway
4. cost, ride
5. choice
6. regular

Day 143
1. The earth shook hard around San Francisco on October 17, 1989.
2. People watching baseball's World **Series** on TV saw it happen.
3. and
4. many
5. days
6. disaster

Day 144
1. Relief gardens, planted during the Great Depression, helped feed people.
2. Victory gardens were planted during **World** War II.
3. enjoy
4. people
5. It's
6. location

ANSWER KEY *(cont.)*

Day 145
1. If you live where there is wind, a windmill may be useful.
2. Some windmills in **Holland** are used to pump up water.
3. were used
4. Many
5. sails
6. unusual

Day 146
1. When May 1 comes, people usually think about flowers.
2. **Known** as May Day, it's when people also think about workers.
3. Chicago
4. workers
5. right
6. factory

Day 147
1. Did you know that people in many countries eat bugs?
2. You might say, "**Yuck**!"
3. are
4. of protein
5. cheap
6. available

Day 148
1. When it wants dinner, the cheetah can't be beat.
2. Found in **Africa**, cheetahs can sprint up to 60 miles (97 kilometers) per hour.
3. can't
4. They
5. prey
6. discovered

Day 149
1. How many pounds of trash do you make each day?
2. People in the United **States** make about four pounds (two kilograms) of waste each day.
3. in the past years
4. recycle
5. throw
6. garbage

Day 150
1. If it is springtime, it may be tornado time.
2. Tornadoes form a lot in the **Midwest** in the spring.
3. A, a
4. tornado, funnel
5. cellar
6. twister

Day 151
1. If you have read fables, you have heard of Aesop.
2. Some people think he was a slave from ancient **Greece**.
3. from many storytellers
4. the
5. moral
6. publish

Day 152
1. Some dogs, such as rescue dogs, are hardworking.
2. **German** shepherds have a good sense of smell.
3. or
4. are
5. site
6. search

Day 153
1. After a lot of use, rubber tires become scrap.
2. In **Florida**, scrap tires were used for an artificial reef.
3. the, tire, a, bad
4. were
5. Now
6. trickiest

Day 154
1. In 1975, everyone wanted to own an unusual pet.
2. Thought up by **Gary** Dahl, the pet was a rock.
3. came
4. in
5. do
6. decoration

Day 155
1. If you look closely, you can see right through this fish.
2. The X-ray tetra is found in the Amazon **River**.
3. fish's
4. You
5. It's
6. aquarium

Day 156
1. If you eat pancakes, you may pour something from a tree on them.
2. You'll see lots of maple trees in **Vermont**.
3. trees
4. and
5. hole
6. collection

© *Shell Education*

ANSWER KEY *(cont.)*

Day 157
1. The Olympic Games, held every four years**,** are fun to watch.
2. They started in ancient **Greece** thousands of years ago.
3. were
4. the
5. by
6. victory

Day 158
1. Have you ever used a typewriter**?**
2. Christopher L. **Sholes** invented a practical typewriter in 1873.
3. a
4. He
5. through
6. description

Day 159
1. For hundreds of years**,** people have loved coffee.
2. **Even** during the Civil War, soldiers wanted coffee.
3. beans
4. Coffee
5. seems
6. available

Day 160
1. If you like to swim**,** you can have fun and stay cool.
2. Jeremiah and Jenna like to swim at the River **City** Water Park.
3. in an inner tube
4. Jenna
5. too
6. weightless

Day 161
1. If you have a big job to do**,** make a plan.
2. Students at **South** Street School planned and planted a big garden.
3. They
4. worked
5. There
6. determined

Day 162
1. If you like beautiful countryside**,** visit Alaska.
2. On **January** 3, 1959, Alaska joined the United States.
3. Alaska, Russia
4. from Russia
5. weather
6. glacier

Day 163
1. Dr. Seuss wrote many books**,** such as <u>Hop on Pop</u>.
2. His full name was Theodor Seuss **Geisel**.
3. books
4. wrote, illustrated
5. by
6. rhyme

Day 164
1. On August 21**,** 1959, the 50th state joined the United States.
2. Made up of islands, Hawaii is in the Pacific **Ocean**.
3. on, of
4. is
5. You'll
6. volcano

Day 165
1. Carson likes to take pictures**,** and Mia likes to make movies.
2. Carson found an old **Kodak** camera in his attic.
3. with their cell phones
4. easily
5. current
6. portrait

Day 166
1. From 1861 to 1865**,** the United States was at war.
2. The Civil **War** had many causes, and slavery was one of them.
3. was
4. Abraham Lincoln
5. died
6. servant

Day 167
1. Do you ever look at the man in the moon**?**
2. A story from **China** tells about a toad in the moon.
3. moon, cheese
4. of cheese
5. there's
6. lunar

Day 168
1. Did you know that our sun is a star**?**
2. It's on the outer part of the Milky **Way** galaxy.
3. The
4. is
5. It's
6. solar

ANSWER KEY (cont.)

Day 169
1. What is your favorite summer holiday**?**
2. The 4th of **July** celebrates America's independence.
3. and
4. Many, ball
5. lightning
6. celebration

Day 170
1. After going to college**,** Ramon knows what he wants to do.
2. Ramon wants to be a conductor on an **Amtrak** train.
3. likes, traveling, seeing
4. new
5. load
6. engineer

Day 171
1. After getting your allowance**,** what do you do next?
2. When he was seven, Ben **Franklin** bought a toy whistle.
3. Franklin
4. the
5. too
6. example

Day 172
1. On June 25, 1894**,** a young mother climbed on her bike and rode away.
2. Leaving **Boston**, Annie Londonderry started biking around the world.
3. but
4. Her
5. ads
6. determined

Day 173
1. In 1985**,** kids could buy the first box of 64 crayons.
2. **The** crayon pack had 13 shades of blue in it.
3. you
4. with glitter
5. choose
6. artist

Day 174
1. When introduced in 1963**,** zip codes first had five numbers.
2. **You** may know that zip stands for zone improvement plan.
3. Some
4. at
5. mail
6. persuade

Day 175
1. In 1982**,** a man attached 42 weather balloons to a lawn chair.
2. Larry Walters, later known as Lawn **Chair** Walters, wanted to fly.
3. balloons
4. Walters
5. fined
6. capable

Day 176
1. At the age of 51**,** Joshua Slocum left the Boston Harbor alone.
2. It was April 24, 1895, and he was in a tiny sloop, *Spray*.
3. returned
4. He
5. feat
6. example

Day 177
1. When summer comes**,** be sure to keep cool.
2. In Death **Valley**, California, the temperature once rose to 134 °F (57 °C)!
3. quickly
4. Hot
5. desert
6. wilderness

Day 178
1. Andy, a polar bear**,** found it hard to keep cool at the zoo.
2. He would get too hot at the Atlanta **Zoo**.
3. gave
4. Andy
5. beat
6. refrigerator

Day 179
1. How would you like to be a treasure hunter**?**
2. Mel Fisher found a sunken **Spanish** ship in 1985.
3. tons
4. and
5. where
6. explore

Day 180
1. In July and August**,** people may say it's the dog days of summer.
2. This phrase is based on **Sirius**, which is also known as the Dog Star.
3. days
4. Romans
5. idle
6. relax

© Shell Education

REFERENCES CITED

Haussamen, Brock. 2014. "Some Questions and Answers About Grammar." Retrieved from http://www.ateg.org/grammar/qna.php.

Hillocks, George, Jr., and Michael W. Smith. 1991. "Grammar and Usage." In *Handbook of Research on Teaching the English Language Arts*. James Flood, Julie M. Jensen, Diane Lapp, and James R. Squire. New York: Macmillan.

Hodges, Richard E. 1991. "The Conventions of Writing." In *Handbook of Research on Teaching the English Language Arts*. James Flood, Julie M. Jensen, Diane Lapp, and James R. Squire. New York: Macmillan.

———. 2003. "Grammar and Literacy Learning." In *Handbook of Research on Teaching the English Language Arts*, 2nd ed. James Flood, Julie M. Jensen, Diane Lapp, and James R. Squire. New York: Macmillan.

Lederer, Richard. 1987. *Anguished English: An Anthology of Accidental Assaults upon Our Language.* New York: Dell.

Marzano, Robert J. 2010. When Practice Makes Perfect. . .Sense. *Educational Leadership* 68(3): 81–83.

Truss, Lynne. 2003. *Eats, Shoots and Leaves: The Zero Tolerance Approach to Punctuation.* New York: Gotham Books.

CONTENTS OF THE DIGITAL RESOURCE CD

Teacher Resources

Resource	Filename
Diagnostic Assessment Directions	directions.pdf
Practice Page Item Analysis	pageitem.pdf pageitem.doc pageitem.xls
Student Item Analysis	studentitem.pdf studentitem.doc studentitem.xls
Standards Chart	standards.pdf

Student Resources

All of the 180 practice pages are contained in a single PDF. In order to print specific days, open the PDF and select the pages to print.

Resource	Filename
Practice Pages Day 1–Day 180	practicepages.pdf

© Shell Education